This
Our Dark
Country

This
Our Dark
Country

THE AMERICAN SETTLERS OF LIBERIA

Catherine Reef

CLARION BOOKS ✚ NEW YORK

PHOTO CREDITS

Mason County Museum, Maysville, Ky.: p. 11
Kendall Whaling Museum: p. 13
Independence National Historical Park: p. 14
John Hartwell Cocke Papers (#640), The Albert and Shirley Small Special Collections Library,
University of Virginia Library: p. 65
The Connecticut Historical Society, Hartford, Conn.: p. 73
From the Collection of Madison County Historical Society, Oneida, N.Y.: p. 74
Tennessee State Museum Collection. Copy photography by June Dorman: p. 93
AP/Wide World Photos: pp. 99, 106, 108, 109, 110
Photo by Ricardo Thomas, The White House: p. 105
All other illustrations are from the collections of the Library of Congress.

Clarion Books
a Houghton Mifflin Company imprint
215 Park Avenue South, New York, NY 10003
Copyright © 2002 by Catherine Reef
Book design by Trish Parcell Watts
Maps on pages 120–121 by Kayley LeFaiver
The text was set in 14.5-point Fournier Monotype.

www.houghtonmifflinbooks.com

Manufactured in China

Library of Congress Cataloging-in-Publication Data
Reef, Catherine.
This our dark country : the American settlers of Liberia / by Catherine Reef.
        p. cm.
Summary: Explores the history of the colony, later the independent nation of Liberia, which was
established on the west coast of Africa in 1822 as a haven for free African Americans.
Includes bibliographical references (p.) and index.
    ISBN 0-618-14785-3
    1. African Americans—Colonization—Liberia—Juvenile literature.   2. Liberia—History—To
1847—Juvenile literature.   3. African Americans—Liberia—History—19th century—Juvenile
literature. [1. African Americans—Colonization—Africa.   2. Liberia—History—To 1847.
3. African Americans—Liberia—History—19th century.   4. Slaves—Emancipation.
5. Antislavery movements.   6. American Colonization Society.]   I. Title
    DT633 .R44 2002
    966.62'04496073—dc21   2002003966

SCP   10 9 8 7 6 5 4 3 2 1

Come hither, son of Afric . . . come;
And o'er the wide and weltering sea,
Behold thy lost yet lovely home,
That fondly waits to welcome thee.

"LIBERIA, HAPPY LAND,"
BY BEVERLY R. WILSON,
NINETEENTH-CENTURY LIBERIAN SETTLER

Contents

———❦———

"These Free, Sunny Shores"

Two long months, and nothing to see but the ocean. At last the voyage was nearing its end, and the view was changing. Nine-year-old Matilda Skipwith stood with her family on the ship's deck and stared at the land. There, in the distance, were the marshy beaches and high inland hills of the colony of Liberia, on the west coast of Africa.

A rumbling startled Matilda's little sister, Felicia, who held their mother's hand. It was the sound of thunder, something the Skipwiths had not heard since leaving Norfolk, Virginia, in early

November. Throughout the journey, the sea had been calm and the skies had been clear. Now it was December 31, 1833, and as the sailing ship *Jupiter* neared its port, dark storm clouds rolled overhead.

On deck were three white missionaries and forty African Americans, among them the eight members of the Skipwith family. Just a few months earlier, the Skipwiths had been slaves, the property of a Virginia planter named John Hartwell Cocke. Now they were free and about to start a new life. Cocke had given them their freedom and paid their passage to Liberia.

Liberia was founded in 1822 so that African Americans might return to the continent of their ancestors. It promised to

An artist's view of Monrovia, Liberia, in the early nineteenth century.

be a place where black Americans could live as equals with their fellow citizens. Liberia was a great experiment. No one knew what would happen when people born and raised in the United States of America went to live in an unsettled region of Africa. Would the colony thrive?

The immigrants aboard the *Jupiter* were embarking on a grand adventure. Like the European settlers who had come to North America in the 1600s, they were building a nation in the wilderness. They were leaving behind one way of life and setting foot in another.

The passengers had sailed away from slavery and prejudice. More than 2 million people of African descent were enslaved in the American South in 1833. Forced to work for the benefit of white owners, most slaves had never tasted freedom. They were denied the right to vote or to move freely in society. Their owners decided what kind of work they would do, where they would live, what they would eat and wear, and whether they could marry. When they got sick, the owners decided if they needed to see a doctor. Enslaved mothers and fathers could not even call their children their own, because slaves were property to be bought and sold. No one knew when a slaveholder might choose to sell some members of a family and keep others. Any slave who broke the rules—who came to work late, moved too slowly, or was caught stealing or trying to run away— risked whipping, branding, or some other brutal punishment.

Most enslaved workers were field hands who raised crops of tobacco, sugar, rice, or cotton. If they lived on a large plantation, as most did, a loud bell or horn awakened them at

"I hope to see the day when Africa . . . shall rise Bud and Blossom as the rose of the garden of life."

THE PARTING "Buy us too."

"Buy us too." A slaveholder with his newly acquired property, a man in chains, rejects pleas from the man's wife, who cannot bear to see her family destroyed.

four A.M. Throughout the long growing season, they had to be in the fields before sunrise to till the soil, sow the seed, nurture the growing plants, or harvest the mature crops. They had to work as hard and as fast as they could on too little sleep and a meager diet. During the harvest, they might work eighteen or twenty hours a day.

No one got off easily. Women with newborn babies had to carry their infants to the field and leave them under a tree during working hours. Old men took care of farm animals or sharpened the master's tools, while aged women watched the children of working mothers or helped out in the kitchen. By the time they were Matilda Skipwith's age, children worked, too. Many nine-year-olds were already going to the fields.

"Little boys, and girls, too, worked and cried, toting brush to the fires, husking the corn, watching the stock, and running out errands for the master and mistress," wrote one man who grew up in slavery. He noted that for all of their hard work, the children received "scoldings and beatings as their reward." Children also looked after younger brothers and sisters, carried water, and swept floors. They waited on the master's family during meals and took out the trash. Enslaved children never went to school.

Plantation owners needed household servants, so some slaves worked as maids or butlers, seamstresses or footmen, laundresses or cooks. Others were trained to be artisans, such as blacksmiths, carpenters, and shoemakers. Usually these workers practiced their trades on the plantation, but sometimes their owners hired them out to work for other people. Matilda's father, Peyton Skipwith, belonged to the population of skilled plantation workers. As a stonemason, he would easily find work helping to build Liberia's capital, Monrovia.

About 319,000 free African Americans also lived in the United States in 1830. Many of these people had been granted independence by their owners, while others had saved enough money to purchase their freedom. Not only did owners frequently allow slave artisans to keep part of their earnings, but some enslaved field hands made money in their spare time by doing odd jobs or raising chickens or vegetables for sale. A number of free African Americans had simply run away from slavery, and some were the sons and daughters of people who had achieved free status. Just as a child born to a slave mother was enslaved, a child born to a free black woman was legally free.

For blacks, being free did not mean having the same rights as whites, though. In many places, and especially in the South, it was against the law for African Americans to move from state to state or county to county. Laws dictated what they could buy or

Liberia's St. Paul River, twenty-five miles from the coast, circa 1900.

sell. They were required to work and pay taxes, but most often they could not vote or send their children to the schools that their taxes supported. And there was always a risk that they might be kidnapped and sold as slaves.

All of that was in the past for the African Americans aboard the *Jupiter*. They planned to live in freedom in a land where manatees swam among the roots of mangrove trees. In Liberia, monkeys and gibbons climbed in the rainforest canopy, pygmy hippopotamuses lazed in rivers, and lemons, limes, and pineapples grew wild. "The quickness and luxuriance of the vegetation in western Africa is such, that without much exaggeration, the plants may be said visibly to grow," wrote an early historian of the region.

Beyond the swampy lowlands of the Liberian coast, a thick forest blanketed hills that rose higher and higher. Narrow streams flowing down from the interior became gushing rivers by the time they reached the ocean. This tropical land had two seasons, rainy and dry. Downpours could last for twelve hours in the rainy season, from April until November. During the dry season, hot Saharan winds blew over the land and parched people's throats.

This section of West Africa had a native population consisting of at least sixteen ethnic groups, all speaking different languages. The Kru people formed one of the largest groups. These coastal people, skilled at sailing and fishing, rowed out in fleets of canoes to greet incoming ships. For many generations,

A Kru village located near Monrovia.

A Mandinka group portrait.

British and American sea captains had hired Kru sailors to work on trading vessels and warships. When their voyages ended, the men went home with some knowledge of English and gifts for the village elders from far-off ports.

The Mandinka, another large ethnic group, traded goods with the other peoples of the region. Mandinka metalsmiths, potters, and weavers crafted beautiful and useful items that were always in demand. The Vai people, like the Mandinka, practiced Islam. At the time Liberia was colonized, the Vai were engaged in the slave trade. The selling of human beings to Europeans was an evil that had flourished along the African coast since the 1400s. White traders captured many slaves for export, but some Africans, such as the Vai, profited by selling enemy prisoners who had been taken in war. They also sold widows, orphans, wrongdoers, and anyone else who was a burden to the community.

The *Jupiter* docked, and the Skipwiths prepared to go ashore. History might well have forgotten these ordinary people, but they wrote letters to the Cocke family and to their own relatives in Virginia, and these letters have survived the passing of time. In the years ahead, the Skipwiths endured illness and hardships. But like thousands of other pioneers in Liberia, they learned to love their rough-hewn land of liberty. Matilda Skipwith wrote as an adult, "I hope to see the day when Africa this our dark Country shall rise Bud and Blossom as the rose of the garden of life."

A man who immigrated to Liberia in 1853 expressed himself more forcefully. He stated that as dear as his wife and two children were to him, "I would rather, if need be, bury them on these free, sunny shores, myself alone at midnight, or trust them in the forest to the tender mercies of the African hyena . . . than to leave them as drudges in America. . . ."

CHAPTER TWO

"Beyond the Reach of Mixture"

Although the United States of America was founded on principles of freedom and equality, from the beginning, many of its people lived in slavery. At the start of the nineteenth century, most Americans were aware of this contrast between the nation's ideals and its practices, but they disagreed about how—or whether—to resolve it.

There were groups that opposed slavery and wanted it done away with. They included the free black population and the aboli-

tionists, both white and black. Their opinions carried little weight, because the whites in power paid scant attention to what African Americans thought and the abolitionist movement was young and still very small.

Then there were the wealthy southern planters who did have clout and who wanted slavery to continue, wrong or right. Slave labor had allowed the South to build a strong economy based on agriculture, and southerners feared that without free labor their plantations would fail.

The prevailing opinion, however, was that of most white Americans, who admitted that slavery was wrong but stopped short of demanding its immediate end. This group included Thomas Jefferson, author of the Declaration of Independence and third president of the United States. "Nothing is more certainly written in the book of fate, than that these people are to be free," Jefferson wrote in 1820. As he saw it, though, there was only one problem: If the slaves were freed, then blacks and whites might mingle in society as equals and possibly marry. This prospect horrified Jefferson, who believed that blacks were "inferior to the whites in the endowments of body and mind." Even though Jefferson had a close relationship with an enslaved woman and probably fathered some of her children, he proposed that African Americans be shipped overseas, "beyond the reach of mixture."

Thomas Jefferson was one of the most famous people to favor sending blacks to a distant colony, but he was not the first. In 1787, some English humanitarians had actually founded

This enslaved woman, named Lucy, was born on Thomas Jefferson's estate, Monticello, around 1811, and sold at public auction in 1827 to George Blatterman of Virginia. In this photograph, taken in the 1840s, Lucy holds Blatterman's granddaughter, Charlotte Elizabeth Blatterman.

such a place: the British colony of Sierra Leone, on the west coast of Africa. The first colonists in Sierra Leone included black men who had fought for the British in the American Revolution in exchange for their freedom, as well as former slaves from Great Britain and Jamaica.

Slaves and free people of African heritage had lived in England since the 1600s. In the mid-seventeenth century, when British planters were using African slaves to build a sugar industry in the colony of Jamaica, England's black population began to rise. Wealthy families bought African children to be playmates for their own offspring and African adults to be domestic servants. Estimates of Britain's black population vary, but most likely it never exceeded ten thousand in the eighteenth century. Britain ended its participation in the slave trade in 1807, and the Emancipation Act of 1833 freed all slaves in Britain and its colonies.

At the time Thomas Jefferson pondered the future of slavery, a small number of American blacks had already been transported across the ocean by Paul Cuffe, a free black man. Cuffe was a rich New England trader who owned a fleet of whaling ships. For years, he had used his wealth and influence for the benefit of others. He had built a school for the children of his hometown, Westport, Massachusetts, and he had joined the abolitionists. Cuffe declared, "As I am of the African race, I feel myself interested for them, and, if I am favored with a talent, I think I am willing that they should be benefitted thereby."

Cuffe visited Sierra Leone in 1811 and seemed to like everything about the place. He found its climate in December healthful and its soil rich. The settlers had built churches and schools, and they took part in the life of the colony as equals to one another. Society recognized their virtues and character rather than their color.

Cuffe was a devout Quaker who was convinced that Christian settlers in Africa would help to end the traffic in slaves. Soon after returning to the United States, he made plans to carry African-American emigrants to Sierra Leone. The outbreak of the War of 1812, a conflict fought largely on the water, forced him to postpone the trip. But in 1815, with the war over, Cuffe set sail from Boston with thirty-eight people and reached Sierra Leone at Christmastime. Thirty of the passengers could not afford to make the trip, so Cuffe paid their way. He asked for nothing in return, saying, "My hope is in a coming day."

Paul Cuffe died in September 1817, before he could transport any more emigrants, but the idea of black colonization remained alive and well.

Whites favored a colony for African Americans for a variety of reasons. Many plantation owners lived in fear of slave revolts, and they worried that free blacks might help their slaves stage uprisings. They therefore wanted the free blacks moved as far away as possible. There were also some people who opposed slavery but supported colonization. They reasoned that planters might be more willing to free their slaves if there were a place to send them. That way, planters could free slaves yet contribute to neither a slave revolt nor a racially mixed society. Finally, clergymen who shared Paul Cuffe's

A silhouette of Paul Cuffe. (Collection of the Kendall Whaling Museum, Sharon Mass.) It was against Cuffe's Quaker beliefs to have his portrait painted, but his faith did allow him to have his shadow traced to create a likeness.

religious goals argued that blacks from the United States would bring to Africa the gifts of Christianity and civilization—as they defined that term.

Whites who supported colonization began to form organizations. In 1815, Ohio citizens formed an antislavery group, the Union Humane Society, and called for African Americans to be relocated to a place in North America beyond the western boundary of white settlement. In the same year, the Kentucky Colonization Society petitioned Congress to set aside a western territory for freed African Americans and to pay to transport them there. Virginia's leaders, meanwhile, wanted the federal government to create a haven for their state's free black population. In 1816, the Virginia Assembly passed a set of resolutions calling on the government to designate land on the Pacific coast for this purpose.

The United States was expanding westward in 1816. Between 1795 and 1810, the number of Americans west of the Appalachian Mountains had grown from 150,000 to more than 1 million. The vast majority of these people lived east of the Mississippi River, though. To the Americans of 1816, the West Coast seemed impossibly remote. Few people foresaw that the Far West would be drawing large numbers of white pioneers by the mid-nineteenth century, or that an African-American colony in that region could only be a temporary solution to the race problem.

The largest and best-known effort to remove African Americans from the United States began in December 1816,

Bushrod Washington, first president of the American Colonization Society, in a portrait by James Sharples, circa 1795–1800.

when a group of whites met in Washington, D.C., to found the American Society for Colonizing the Free People of Color of the United States. This organization, soon known as the American Colonization Society, was the idea of the Reverend Robert Finley, president of the University of Georgia. Finley had brought together some prominent people, among them Francis Scott Key, author of "The Star-Spangled Banner," and Henry Clay, a Kentucky congressman who had helped to negotiate the treaty ending the War of 1812. The society elected George Washington's nephew, Bushrod Washington, to be its president. Since 1799, Bushrod Washington had been a justice of the Supreme Court.

At first, the American Colonization Society sought to create a colony for free blacks either in Africa or in the American wilderness. "They can never enjoy equality among the whites in America; only in a district by themselves will they ever be happy," said Elias B. Caldwell, the society's secretary, who was also a clerk of the Supreme Court. It would cost more to ship people to Africa than to move them onto unsettled American land, but to Caldwell the extra expense would be money well spent. He persuaded the others that blacks relocated to a place in North America might ally themselves with Mexico, Canada, or the Indian nations and make war against the United States. To him there was a danger, too, that the African Americans might harbor fugitives and runaway slaves.

Transportation costs could be met if private citizens made donations. Also, there were many free blacks who had pros-

Elias Boudinot Caldwell, secretary of the American Colonization Society.

pered in trades. These skilled artisans could easily afford a journey across the Atlantic. Africa, then, the members agreed, was the destination of choice.

Although the founders of the American Colonization Society called themselves "men of virtue, piety, and reflection," they danced around the touchy issue of abolishing slavery. Bushrod Washington, Henry Clay, and other members owned slaves themselves and were unwilling to give up this valuable property. The group therefore focused its efforts on colonizing African Americans who were already free.

In borrowing words suggestive of the New Testament, the men of the American Colonization Society congratulated one

Thirty dollars bought a lifetime membership in the American Colonization Society and a certificate like this one.

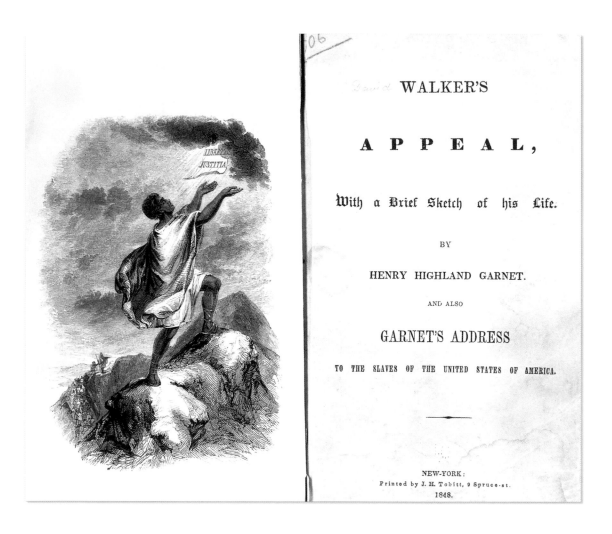

WALKER'S

APPEAL,

With a Brief Sketch of his Life.

BY

HENRY HIGHLAND GARNET.

AND ALSO

GARNET'S ADDRESS

TO THE SLAVES OF THE UNITED STATES OF AMERICA.

NEW-YORK:
Printed by J. H. Tobitt, 9 Spruce-st.
1848.

The frontispiece and title page of the 1848 edition of Walker's Appeal.

another for promoting "peace on earth and good will to man." Elias B. Caldwell listed the benefits that the society's colony would offer to settlers: social equality, houses and land, and transportation overseas. He predicted that free people of color would soon be clamoring to leave the United States.

How wrong he was! Few of the leading African Americans shared Paul Cuffe's eagerness to give people a new life in Africa. In fact, nearly all of them had something to say against colonization. In 1817, the Reverend Richard Allen and James

Forten organized three thousand of Philadelphia's free African Americans in protest. Allen was the first bishop of the African Methodist Episcopal Church, which had been founded to allow African Americans equality in worship. Forten was an outspoken abolitionist. Under the leadership of these two men, the group issued a statement asking the "Humane and Benevolent Inhabitants of Philadelphia" to take no part in any colonization plans. The work of the American Colonization Society, they said, was an "outrage, having no other object in view than the benefit of the slaveholding interests of the country."

Throughout the 1820s, African Americans denounced colonization in Baltimore, Pittsburgh, Boston, and other cities. The strongest condemnation came from David Walker, who was one of Boston's leading abolitionists. In September 1829, he published *Walker's Appeal,* an angry pamphlet that urged slaves to revolt against their masters. In its pages Walker also took aim at colonization. "America is more our country than it is the whites—we have enriched it with our blood and tears," he wrote. "[W]ill they drive us from our property and homes, which we have earned with our blood?"

Slavery's enemies smuggled many copies of *Walker's Appeal* into the South, where its call to rebellion struck fear in the hearts of slaveholders. When it came to colonization, though, Walker was railing against an accomplished fact. The American Colonization Society's settlement had been thriving on the west coast of Africa since 1822, thanks to the president of the United States.

Divine Providence

In 1819, President James Monroe had his own reason for wanting a black colony: He needed a place where he could send Africans rescued from slave ships. Although it had been illegal to import slaves since 1809, some traders had been defying the law and bringing them into the United States anyway. For that reason, on March 3, 1819, Congress passed a law authorizing the navy to stop any ship employing U.S. citizens in the slave trade and to seize any black prisoners on board. The law required the president to resettle the prisoners "beyond the limits of the United States," in Africa.

Returning the prisoners to their own communities was nearly impossible, because the Africans, sometimes those aboard the same ship, came from many different places. Even though most were from west-central Africa, their villages might have been hundreds of miles apart. People from the Sudanese grasslands east of the Sahara Desert and from far-off Mozambique and Madagascar were sold into slavery as well. The prisoners spoke many languages, but usually not English, the one that would have allowed them to communicate with U.S. authorities. Also, most had never seen a map of Africa and would have been unable to pinpoint their homes.

That summer Monroe met with a committee from the American Colonization Society and worked out a deal. It was agreed that the society would take in the rescued Africans. In return, the government would put up housing in the African colony for three hundred people and outfit the first settlers with things they would need to survive in the wilderness. Neither the president nor the colonizationists thought seriously about sending people to Sierra Leone. They intended to create an American colony, of blacks governed by whites. Once the colony was established, some Africans removed from slave ships would join its population.

The government and the American Colonization Society worked out this arrangement even though the African colony did not yet exist. The society had failed to raise enough money to acquire land or send any ships or people overseas. But once the president's offer removed the financial barrier, things began to happen fast. A federal agent chartered a ship, the *Elizabeth*, which was about the size of a modern ferryboat. By January 31, 1820, the *Elizabeth* was docked in New York City, its cargo hold packed with supplies bought with government funds. There were tools, lumber, nails, wheelbarrows, farming implements, a fishing net, and guns and ammunition. Aboard the ship were eighty-eight free African Americans, including thirty-seven children. Despite the protests from Richard Allen and other African-American leaders, some free blacks preferred to leave the United States rather than fight what they believed was a losing battle for equality.

Making the journey were farmers and carpenters, a blacksmith, a seamstress, a shoemaker, and a teacher. One of the travelers was David Lee of Virginia, fifty-five years old and well-off. Unable to convince his grown children to accompany him, he had paid for some of his friends to come along. Aboard ship as well were Elijah Johnson, a New Yorker who had fought in the War of 1812, and Daniel Coker, a thirty-five-year-old minister from Baltimore whose wife and children were to sail to Africa on a later voyage. The passengers also included three agents of the American Colonization Society, government representatives, and two dogs. One of the dogs belonged to an emigrant named Peter Small, and the other was the pet of the ship's crew.

Things went wrong on the voyage right from the start. First, the *Elizabeth* became icebound and could not move. Then, as the ship sat frozen in port, constables came aboard and arrested two passengers for theft. At last, on February 6, the ice that covered the Hudson River began to break up, and the ship headed

"Oh! my soul, what is God about to do for Africa? Surely something great."

for the open ocean. On February 9, as rough weather made almost everyone on board seasick, Daniel Coker, the Baltimore minister, jotted in his journal some lines from an eighteenth-century hymn:

God moves in a mysterious way,
His wonders to perform,
He plants his footsteps in the sea;
And rides upon the storm.

By February 19, the passengers had developed sea legs, and with high hopes they talked about the future. As Daniel Coker stood at the stern, staring into the ship's wake, he thought, "Oh! my soul, what is God about to do for Africa? Surely something great."

All was peaceful on the *Elizabeth* until the eighteenth day at sea, when the dogs got into a vicious fight. The captain lost his temper and called for his pistols, threatening to shoot Peter Small. A government agent calmed the captain and Small's life was spared, but the dogs were thrown overboard and drowned.

The *Elizabeth* anchored at Freetown, Sierra Leone, on March 9. The Americans felt strong emotions as they looked upon Africa and the African people for the first time. Daniel Coker wrote that after meeting some Kru men who had rowed out to greet the ship, "I stood on deck and looked at these children of nature, till streams of tears ran down my cheeks." Gazing toward land, Coker saw several ships that had been seized by the British for trading illegally in slaves. "The sight of them

pained my heart, and made me glad," Coker stated. He explained, "I was pained to find that the slave trade was still carried on, as it appears, even to a great extent; and pleased to find that the British government was using such vigilance in endeavouring to stop it. . . ."

The passengers met some of the people who had gone to Africa with Paul Cuffe, and a local minister invited Daniel Coker to dinner. After enjoying a rich meal that included beef, mutton, pork, fowl, oysters, fish, and an assortment of vegetables, Coker concluded, "[N]one but those who have seen the like, could have believed that such a table could have been furnished with the productions of the soil of Africa."

Women walk past the U.S. consulate in Freetown, Sierra Leone, circa 1900.

On March 17, the ship headed for Sherbro Island, off the coast of Sierra Leone, the site chosen for the new colony. Coker cried out, "Had we about ten thousand of our coloured people from America, here, what might we not do!" He envisioned American colonists building a model nation, converting Africans to Christianity, and rescuing captives from the slave trade.

Coker ended his journal at this point, and soon he lost heart. Swampy Sherbro Island turned out to be a breeding ground for tropical diseases, and within three weeks, twenty-two African-American settlers and all three agents of the American Colonization Society had died of yellow fever. In November, everyone who was left alive abandoned the island and returned to Freetown.

The American Colonization Society sent a second group of agents and settlers to Africa in 1821, and Daniel Coker was reunited with his family. The new agents decided to locate the colony south of Sierra Leone, on a finger of land reaching into the Atlantic Ocean known as Cape Mesurado (sometimes called Cape Montserado or Montserrado). They met with one of the region's native leaders, a man whom the Europeans called King Peter. He agreed—when an agent held a gun to his head—to sell 4,200 square miles to the American Colonization Society for rum, clothing, mirrors, silverware, wineglasses, firearms, and other goods, all worth about $300. He never would be paid in full.

Most of the surviving Sherbro Island settlers moved to Cape Mesurado. (A few Americans, including the Cokers, refused to

leave Sierra Leone.) On April 25, 1822, the Cape Mesurado pioneers raised the American flag and held a formal ceremony of thanksgiving. They named their colony Liberia, for liberty, and optimistically set to work clearing land and building shelters for themselves and future immigrants. The town to be built on Cape Mesurado would be called Monrovia, after President Monroe.

The American pioneers in Africa faced hardships for which they were unprepared. With no crops planted and no shops or markets, they continually coped with shortages. They waited for ships to bring food and supplies from the United States, but the ships never came often enough. Also, because the Americans reached Cape Mesurado just as the rainy season began, construction proceeded slowly. New settlers arrived to discover that their homes had yet to be built, or that they were expected to sleep in a communal shelter with no roof and a muddy floor. "I. may state to you. that I. am much deceiv'd, with, this Country,"

An early view of Cape Mesurado and the houses of Monrovia. Kru fishing boats float along the shoreline; look closely to see a Kru village tucked into the foliage in the foreground.

wrote one disappointed newcomer, Mars Lucas, to his old master in Virginia, "the reports, is all a lie, mearly to Encourage people. to come to this Country. Times is very hard. out. here. every thing is very Dear. and not to be had."

Conditions were so miserable that Dr. Eli Ayres, the white agent in charge of the settlement, tried to convince the colonists to return to Sierra Leone. But Elijah Johnson, the War of 1812 veteran who had sailed on the *Elizabeth*, revived the settlers' courage by responding, "Two years long have I sought a home; here I found one; here I remain." Ayres, who lacked the immigrants' determination, hopped aboard a ship that was sailing back to the United States as soon as he had the chance.

American Colonization Society agent Jehudi Ashmun.

On August 9, 1822, the good ship *Strong* brought to Liberia another group of settlers, accompanied by a twenty-eight-year-old agent of the American Colonization Society named Jehudi Ashmun and his wife. When Ashmun learned that Dr. Ayres had abandoned the colony, he immediately assumed command. The zealous Ashmun knew less about surviving in the African wilderness than the colonists did, but like most white Americans in the early nineteenth century, he took it for granted that blacks needed white supervision. The African Americans in Liberia accepted Ashmun's leadership whether they wanted it or not, because the American Colonization Society governed the colony, and they depended on the society for needed supplies. Mostly, though, they put their faith in Heaven and relied on Divine Providence, God's care and protection.

The settlers and the Ashmuns understood very little about this land called Liberia or its inhabitants. They did not know, for example, that the Africans had ideas about land ownership that were altogether different from those held by white and black Americans. The Africans, like the Native Americans, viewed the earth as something sacred that could not be bought or sold. The residents of an African village lived and worked together on land that had nurtured their parents and grandparents.

As the newcomers asserted power over Cape Mesurado and prepared to expand their holdings, some local chiefs grew alarmed. The most powerful was the leader of the Dei people, called King George by the Americans, who claimed the right to rule northern Cape Mesurado. On November 11, 1822, King George's followers attacked with spears and muskets. Jehudi Ashmun described the African warriors as eight hundred men "pressed shoulder to shoulder, in so compact a form that a child might easily walk upon their heads from one end of the mass to the other." The colonial fighting force numbered thirty-five.

The Africans went after men, women, and children. Jane Hawkins, thirty-nine years old, received thirteen stab wounds and was left for dead—but she survived. Another woman, Minty Draper, was wounded in the head as she ran toward safety with her two young children. She eventually recovered, but the Africans kidnapped the children and held them for seven months.

The Africans, however, were taken aback by what Ashmun called "the destructive power of the machinery of modern warfare": a cannon mounted on a wooden platform. Several volleys from the cannon killed an unknown number of Africans and persuaded the rest to retreat. Then the colonists, in a "state of utter abandonment and solitude," built a barricade around their homes.

This fortification served them well on December 1, when King George attacked again and a thousand African warriors engaged the Americans in battle. The Africans trampled young crops and looted and burned homes as the settlers huddled behind the barricade and fought back. According to legend, a

The slave trade broke up families in Africa just as it did in the United States. Here a woman laments as her child is led to the ship that will carry him to enslavement in the New World.

widow named Matilda Newport used the pipe she was smoking to fire the cannon and protect the settlement. Whether or not the story is true, it was lucky for the Americans that the crew of a British warship sailing along the coast heard the gunfire and came to their aid. The British persuaded the Africans to agree to an uneasy truce, though there would be further outbreaks of fighting in the months and years ahead.

Sometimes, the Americans fired the first shots in these skirmishes in order to disrupt the continuing traffic in slaves. A number of European slave traders were so brazen that they did business in plain view of Cape Mesurado colonists standing on the shore. Beginning in August 1825, Jehudi Ashmun led the settlers in raids on coastal slave stations. The colonists freed some people about to be loaded onto slave ships, and Ashmun secured promises from several local chiefs to give up the slave trade. But this commerce was highly profitable, and it would continue as long as there was a demand for slaves in the New World.

The settlers were also unprepared for the diseases of tropical West Africa. Death visited them frequently in the form of "African fever," or malaria, which is transmitted by mosquitoes. Malaria brings on chills and fever, and it claimed many lives in the nineteenth century. At that time, no one knew what caused it or how to treat it. The colonists blamed it on exposure to sewage or swamp gases, on being drunk, overeating, or having too much time on one's hands. They brewed herb teas in the hope of a cure, but these did little more than quench the thirst. More than one fifth of the settlers died of malaria or other trop-

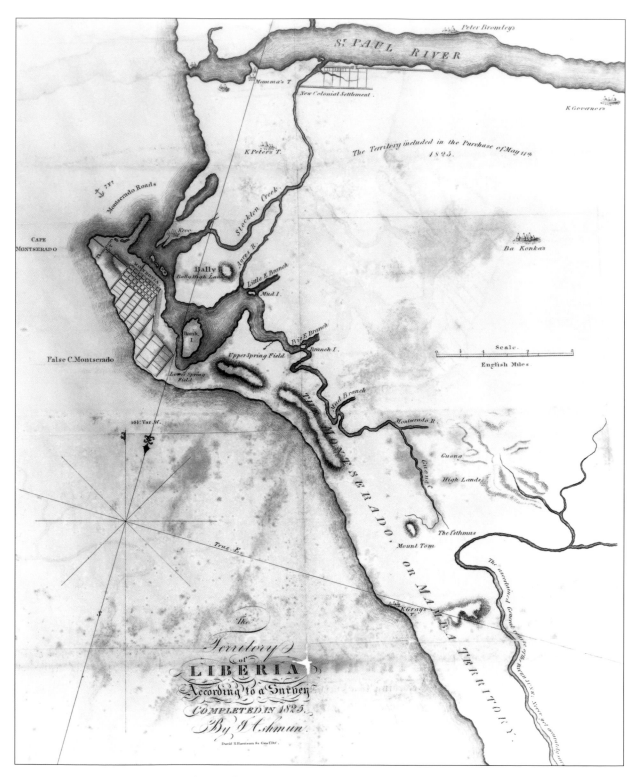

An 1825 map of Liberia drawn from information provided by Jehudi Ashmun. (See pages 120–21 for additional maps.)

ical diseases within a year of their arrival in Africa. Six-year-old Felicia Skipwith, her mother, and her brother Napoleon all died of malaria in 1834.

Between 1820 and 1843, the year of the first Liberian census, seventy-four colonists died in battles with the Africans, sixty-seven drowned, thirteen women died in childbirth, and thirty-six people died of "old age." Disease, however, caused the greatest number of deaths by far: at least eighteen hundred.

The settlers called the health problems that they suffered during their first months in Africa "seasoning," and insisted that the body needed time to adjust to the land and its climate. And indeed, statistics support their claim. The death rate for immigrants spending their first year in Liberia was 21.4 percent; among those who had survived two years in the colony, the death rate was much lower, 3.4 percent.

"Liberia, like all other countries, is not a paradise," wrote the Reverend Samuel Williams, an African American who spent four years there. "It has its sweets and its bitters, its sorrows and its pleasures, its life and its death." At least in Liberia's early years, the sorrows far outnumbered the pleasures. Still, most settlers were determined to put up with the hardships and make the colony succeed. The American Colonization Society acquired more land, driving hard bargains with the native people and often cheating them out of what they were owed. The colonists built villages, and more settlers came. Some state colonization societies built communities in Liberia for African Americans from their own states. The Young Men's Colonization Society of Pennsylvania, for example, founded the coastal

Cape Palmas, site of the settlement founded by the Maryland Colonization Society.

town of Bassa Cove in 1834. Similarly, the Sinoe settlement was for emigrants from Mississippi. The largest state settlement was established by the Maryland Colonization Society in 1831. Known as Maryland in Liberia, it was located more than two hundred miles south of Monrovia, at Cape Palmas.

Until 1827, the American Colonization Society transported only free African Americans who traveled to Liberia voluntarily. After that year, the ships also carried newly emancipated slaves who, although free, had no choice about going. Frugal southern planters had figured out that they could get rid of old and unproductive slaves by sending them to Liberia. Of course, kinder masters such as John Hartwell Cocke were freeing younger, healthy people and sending them to the colony as a reward for loyal service. Robert E. Lee, who later was the great Confederate general, freed his slaves in 1853 and offered to send them to Liberia. Only one family, William C. and Rosabella Burke and their four children, chose to emigrate. By 1827, Africans rescued from slave ships were arriving in Liberia, too. The colonists called them "recaptureds" or "Congoes."

Emigrants from Arkansas are sheltered at the Mount Olivet Baptist Church in New York City while they await passage to Liberia.

There was even a white man who sought racial equality in Liberia. James Richardson's wife had one African-American grandparent. "We have been married five years and have two children, who being only one-eighth African, are blue-eyed, and flaxen haired; and nearly as 'pale-faced' as myself," Richardson wrote to the American Colonization Society in 1832. "Still, they are *coloured* and that is a word with tremendous import in North America!"

Throughout much of the English-speaking world, people like Richardson's children, who had a black great-grandparent, were labeled octoroons. Even people with only a few drops of African blood commonly felt the pain of prejudice in nineteenth-century America. For that reason, some Americans of African heritage who were white in appearance cut their ties to the United States. They joined the free blacks and former slaves who were building the colony of Liberia.

Americans

By the 1840s, Monrovia was a town where streets crossed one another at right angles to form city blocks. The blocks had been divided into quarter-acre plots, and on each one stood a small wooden house. "The neatly painted white cottages, in the style of the southern States, look a little out of place in their surroundings of banana and orange," noted an American traveler in West Africa, "yet they are no doubt cool and comfortable to the occupants."

The coastal settlers were of African ancestry, but they remained Americans. They re-created American life in Africa to the

extent that this was possible. Despite the tropical heat, the settlers wore the same kinds of clothing that other nineteenth-century Americans wore. Men dressed in long pants, vests, jackets, and top hats. Women wore high collars, long sleeves, and skirts that covered their ankles.

The American Colonization Society assigned each household one city plot and some rocky land outside the town limits for farming. The society supported settlers during their first six months in the colony; after that, people had to earn their own living.

Most of Liberia's best-educated settlers and skilled artisans lived in Monrovia, the busiest port. Those who had a talent for business earned a tidy profit trading in African goods. One such person was Joseph Jenkins Roberts. In 1829, at age twenty, Roberts immigrated to Liberia with his widowed mother, four brothers, and two sisters. He went into business with a friend back home in Petersburg, Virginia, supplying the American market with animal hides, ivory, and the hard red wood of the camwood tree. Roberts earned enough money to finance his brother Henry's training in medicine at the Berkshire Medical School in Massachusetts. Henry Roberts returned to Liberia when his education was complete, and for many years he practiced medicine in Monrovia. Liberia needed doctors to combat all the sickness.

Well-dressed settlers gather for a picnic.

A warehouse on the Monrovia waterfront belonging to the American Colonization Society.

While traders like Joseph Jenkins Roberts grew wealthy, Peyton Skipwith, his nephew James, and other artisans were sometimes paid in goods instead of cash for their labor. James Skipwith stacked and mortared so many stones that he felt he was building "the walls of Jerusalem." Yet he wrote that all the hard work was worthwhile, that Liberia "is the Best Country for the Black man that is to be found on the face of the Earth."

Even with money, though, there was little to buy. Every vessel sailing to the United States carried letters from settlers to former owners or the American Colonization Society asking for needed items. People wanted spools of cotton thread for weaving and quills and ink for writing. They requested mules and horses for farming, although these animals seldom thrived in West Africa. Like humans, they were often felled by tropical diseases.

A colonist named James C. Minor sent his old master a shopping list of things that he desired: "pork, beef, . . . mackerel, herrings, . . . codfish, soap, tea, coffee, butter, lard, dry goods, . . . shoes, stockings, table knives and forks, bonnet ribbons, . . . pins, needles, toothbrushes. . . ."

Many of the letter writers mentioned the Almighty. "God

A Methodist church. Stone was a more practical building material than wood. Wooden structures deteriorated quickly in Liberia due to a lack of paint, the humid climate, and a large termite population.

intended Africa for the Black race," James Skipwith wrote. The settlers were religious people who built churches as soon as they completed their homes. They were also great joiners, forming social and charitable groups to promote values that would advance their society. They formed professional groups such as the Liberian Agricultural Society, which encouraged people to farm. Men joined the Freemasons and other fraternal orders, while their wives belonged to the Ladies Benevolent Society of Monrovia. This organization aided the many children whose parents had died of African fever. The Ladies Dorcas Society, which was founded in 1843 by the Methodist Episcopal Church of Monrovia, built an institution to house the poor. (Dorcas is the name of a character in the Bible known for her acts of charity.) Every settlement had poor, sick, orphaned, or widowed residents who survived only with aid from their neighbors.

Among the people needing assistance was Jane Hawkins, the woman stabbed by Africans in November 1822, whose injuries had left her disabled. In 1836, she wrote in a letter to the American Colonization Society, "Our house scarcely shelters us from the torrents of rain which fall during the wet season & but for the occasional help of those who remember the poor among us, we should not have even so much of the common necessaries of life as to sustain nature!"

Groups such as the Daughters of Temperance urged people to abstain from drinking alcohol. Many settlers agreed with the American Colonization Society that drunkenness was a public nuisance and a moral evil. The American Colonization Society approved of alcohol only for medical use and required all merchants selling rum and other spirits to pay an annual fee of twenty-five dollars.

The colonists joined charities and clubs to do good, but they also took great pleasure in the pomp and ceremony that membership entailed. They wore uniforms and badges, gave speeches, and marched in elaborate parades. Meetings usually began with a procession and a flowery oration. After prayers and music, the members socialized over refreshments.

Some groups, such as the Ladies Liberia Literacy Institute, had educational goals. Illiteracy was widespread among adults in the young colony, because it was a crime in the southern United States to teach a slave to read or write. The fact that a handful of slaveholders broke this law accounts for the ability of the Skipwiths and some others to express themselves on paper.

The Americans in Liberia built schools for their children even though few qualified teachers had immigrated. The schools operated on the Lancasterian system, which was devised around 1800 by the English schoolmaster Joseph Lancaster. Lancasterian schools relied on advanced students, called monitors, to teach some lessons to the beginners and to correct their behavior. In this way, one teacher could oversee the education of many youngsters.

The American colonists founded Liberia on principles of equality and justice. "Here we enjoy the same rights and priviledges that the white brethren does in America," wrote one former slave. Yet they often denied those rights and privileges to others, including the Africans recaptured from slave ships. Neither the American Colonization Society nor the settlers

"I wonder to think that a people who themselves have but just been redeemed from fetters should . . . look with an evil eye upon the freedom of others. . . ."

American naval vessels seize a slave ship off the coast of Cuba. Liberia had agreed to take in Africans liberated from ships such as this one.

attempted to return the recaptured people to their homelands. Liberia became the recaptureds' home, but they and the American-born settlers lived by different rules.

By 1843, a total of 287 recaptured people had been taken to Liberia. As soon as they arrived, the colony's leaders began stripping away their African identity. The recaptureds were given American-sounding names and American-style clothing to wear. They were instructed in the doctrines of Christianity and told when to pray, when to wake up in the morning, and when to go to sleep at night. Laws barred them from mingling with the native African population, although some recaptured men ignored this rule and chose wives from nearby African villages.

Many of the recaptureds were forced into apprenticeship. Legal agreements bound them to work for settlers for seven years, or until age twenty-one if they were children. Others went to live in the settlement of New Georgia, where they raised crops to feed the people of Monrovia. In the spring of 1840, Captain Charles H. Bell of the United States Navy visited New Georgia. He saw a little town where wood-framed houses lined two main streets. The residents, Bell noted, "call themselves *Americans.*" He observed that they "all take great pride in imitating the customs and manners of those who are more civilized, having furniture in their houses, and many comforts they never dreamt of in their own country." It never occurred to most nineteenth-century Americans that an African culture could be as civilized as their own.

To assume that all the recaptured people were as happy and industrious as Bell portrayed them, however, would be a mistake. Some tried to go back to the lands of their birth and failed, and some committed suicide.

The recaptureds were small in number and cut off from their geographical and cultural roots, so it was possible to bring most of them into settler society. The native people of the region were more resistant to change. There were many more of them, and they lived in long-established villages under the rule of powerful chiefs.

Some aspects of traditional African life disturbed the citizens of Monrovia and other coastal towns. To the Christian settlers, the Africans held false religious beliefs. While some African ethnic groups practiced Islam, others had faith in powerful gods that lived in nature. (The idea that trees, rocks, and other natural objects have souls or consciousness is called *animism*.) Also, the West Africans interacted closely with the spirit world. They believed that the gods of the forest entered their bodies during religious rituals, and that the ghosts of their

A group portrait of native men of various ethnic groups of Liberia. The American settlers disapproved of the native people's relative nakedness.

ancestors brought them good luck or misfortune. Most distressing, though, was the Africans' belief in witchcraft and magic, which the colonists called the work of the Devil.

It shocked the immigrants that most West Africans wore very little clothing. Men of the Kru and other ethnic groups wore a single garment, a cloth wrapped around the loins, and adorned themselves with face paint and tattoos. Women's breasts usually were bare. A law that required all Africans living within colonial settlements to be fully clothed or pay a fine protected the disapproving colonists from the sight of African bodies. Another thing that offended the settlers was the custom of African men to have several wives. The men of West Africa measured their wealth in cattle and women.

Like the American colonists, the native Africans were obligated by law to pay taxes or work on roads or other public projects. Unlike the settlers, the native people were denied the right to vote. And Africans who ran afoul of the law were punished with whipping.

In 1840, a new immigrant in Monrovia was horrified to hear other colonists say that "the best way to civilize these Natives is with [gun]powder and ball." The newcomer remarked, "I wonder to think that a people who themselves have but just been redeemed from fetters should . . . look with an evil eye upon the freedom of others. . . ."

In Liberia, the African-American colonists created a society in which some people had more rights than others. Instead of embracing the Africans as equals, they stood back, straightened their stiff collars, and looked down their noses at these "savages" and "heathens." Like most white Americans of the nineteenth century, they considered themselves superior to people who were not Christian and who were less technologically advanced. Peyton Skipwith spoke for many when he stated, "It is something strange to think that these people of Africa are called our ancestors. In my present thinking if we have any ancestors they could not have been like these hostile tribes. . . ."

CHAPTER FIVE

Life Upriver

A two-masted sailing vessel, the *Hunter*, reached Liberia on March 13, 1825, carrying sixty-six immigrants from Virginia, North Carolina, and the District of Columbia. Jehudi Ashmun led this band of pioneers inland to a site alongside the St. Paul River where periodic floods blanketed the earth with nutrient-rich silt. There, where the soil was loose, black, and free of stones, he directed the people to build the farming community of Caldwell. Ashmun named the town for Elias B. Caldwell, the first secretary of the American Colonization Society.

The society encouraged Liberia's settlers to farm in order to be self-sufficient. The colony would succeed only if the people grew enough food for themselves and developed some crops for export. Most of the colonists preferred to do just about anything *except* farm to earn their living, because farming had been the work of slaves in the United States. As a result, too many settlers depended for food on shipments from the United States and trade with the Africans. If bad weather delayed the ships, or if the Africans withheld their goods, people might go hungry. "The cultivation of your rich lands, is the only way you will ever find out to independence, comfort and wealth," Ashmun advised the people of Caldwell.

A home on the St. Paul River.

Jehudi Ashmun gave strict orders for the development of Caldwell. He directed the settlers to clear away the dense jungle growth between their assigned lots and the river, pointing out which shade trees to cut down and which to leave standing. Clearing the land was treacherous work. Tall trees had to be felled with axes, and saplings cut even with the ground. Bushes and vines were cut away using sharp, curved blades known as billhooks. As they labored, the builders of Caldwell had to remain alert for scorpions and insects on the jungle floor and pythons in the branches overhead.

Ashmun organized elections for local officials, including a

Milking the goat: a three-person job. The child at right wears an African cap, a clue that he might have been African-born and adopted by this settler woman's family.

In this watercolor painted between 1808 and 1816, a Jamaican woman pounds cassava in preparation for cooking. Portuguese traders introduced cassava, which is native to the American tropics, to Africa in the sixteenth century.

magistrate and a head farmer. He ordered all males sixteen and older to join a militia to protect the community from possible attack. And he forbade the residents to leave town to trade with the native people. Everyone living in Caldwell was required to farm.

Growing conditions in West Africa were so different from those in North America that even colonists who had been farmers in the United States had to learn from scratch how to raise crops in Liberia. In America, farmers planted in the spring, tended their growing plants through the hot summer, and harvested in the fall as temperatures dropped. But Liberia had no true spring, summer, or fall. It was hot all year long, and the deluges of the rainy season washed away seedlings. Wheat, apples, and other popular North American crops did poorly in the heat and humidity of Liberia.

The American Colonization Society counseled settlers to follow the example of African farmers and plant rice, yams, plantains, and cassava. Cassava, which was sometimes called cassada in the nineteenth century, is a tropical plant with starchy roots that is used to make tapioca.

Youngsters adapted easily to the African diet. "For four or

five months after we arrived in Africa, my children looked better than I ever saw them," wrote William C. Burke to his former owner, Robert E. Lee. "They were so fond of palm oil and rice, and eat so much of it, that they fattened very fast." Adults often had a harder time getting used to these strange new African foods. Cassava, one immigrant complained, "is a coarse, tough, clammy, tasteless root, which nothing but dire necessity would induce a man to eat." Some people experimented to discover whether their favorite vegetables and fruits would flourish in Caldwell's soil.

The most successful crop grown for export was coffee, which already grew wild in West Africa. Planters preferred to raise a variety of coffee that they called Liberica, which thrived on mountainsides or on coastal flatlands and resisted disease. "Millions of coffee trees of sufficient sizes and ages may be gathered from the woods," noted an editorial in the *Liberia Herald* in 1837; "we know from experiment that they will bear in three years from the time of transplantation, so that a man who will commence with spirit and set out fifteen or twenty thousand plants, may calculate, with a good degree of certainty, on a large quantity of coffee, in three years from the time he commences operation." Liberian farmers insisted that Liberica coffee lost its fine flavor when the trees were transplanted to Sierra Leone or other nearby regions.

The other important export crop was sugar. By 1863, Liberia was exporting two thousand pounds of sugar annually to the nearby British colonies of Sierra Leone, Gold Coast (in present-day Ghana), and Lagos (the capital of modern Nige-

An upriver coffee plantation.

ria). They also exported fifty thousand pounds annually to the United States. Some farmers let their sugar cane ferment and distilled its juice to make rum. They sold this rum, or "cane juice," in Liberia, despite the government's antidrinking policy. The sugar trade gave rise to another upriver industry, the making of barrels from native wood and vines to hold the exported sugar cane.

Caldwell was a well-established town in 1840, when four Kru men pulled a barge carrying Captain Bell of the U.S. Navy up the St. Paul River. "Here are a number of farms delightfully situated," wrote Bell, describing Caldwell. "Near the banks of the river is an avenue opened, extending in a straight line for six miles, lined with plantain, banana, and orange trees. On this road, the farms, each of ten acres, are situated; having comfortable dwellings, and cultivated with cassada, Indian corn, rice and sweet potatoes."

Bell tried to capture in words the grandeur of the upriver scenery: "The ground is undulating, elevated from ten to fifteen feet above the water, and commanding beautiful views of the river and opposite banks, which are nearly three quarters of a mile distant, and enjoying the sea breeze throughout the day."

In 1828, the colonists had built a second farming community on the St. Paul River and given it the American-style name Millsburg. This town was twenty miles inland, as far into the back country as the Liberians' boats could safely navigate.

Still, curiosity lured some people deeper into the wilderness. One such person was Reuben Dongey, a freeborn black from Virginia, who arrived in Monrovia in 1824, at age thirty-seven. Dongey heard African traders talk about the distant town of Bopolu, whose name meant "beyond the hills," a place that no settler had ever seen. Traders from diverse African ethnic groups came together at Bopolu to buy and sell their wares. A wise Mandinka chief named Sao Boso ruled Bopolu and controlled African trade from the interior to the coast. Sao Boso was a skilled politician and a savvy businessman who befriended other African leaders. He prevailed on his friends to live in peace with the American colony.

In 1828, Reuben Dongey and three companions set off to find Bopolu and meet Sao Boso. They traveled by river as far as they could, navigating rapids and making their way around waterfalls. Then they moved by foot through thick vegetation for twenty-five miles until they spotted Bopolu amid the rolling

"The ground is undulating, elevated from ten to fifteen feet above the water, and commanding beautiful views of the river and opposite banks...."

hills. Upon returning to Monrovia, Dongey reported to colonial leaders that the African town "contains more than 1000 houses, and is well fortified with a barricade, and 8,000 men armed with muskets, can be brought to its defence." He communicated Sao Boso's wish to create a direct path for commerce between the trading center and the settlers. An American Colonization Society agent hired a native African crew to build a road connecting Bopolu and Millsburg, and by 1830, this road was heavily traveled.

The upriver settlers enjoyed peace until 1836, when they were caught in the middle of a long, violent African power struggle. Sao Boso had died, and the region's other chiefs fought one another, each determined to be the most powerful person in the region. Upriver settlers heard cries of "War! war's come," as Getumbe, a chief of the inland Gola people, made a show of power by attacking Millsburg in December 1839. The local militia defended the town and prevented any loss of life, but Getumbe's army wounded several colonists, took six prisoners, and looted a farm. In communication with the colonial leaders, Getumbe denied responsibility for the assault and insisted it was the work of mischief makers.

Jehudi Ashmun was also gone, having died in 1828, and a series of white governors had taken his place. The governor of Liberia at the time of the attack was Thomas Buchanan, whom the settlers had nicknamed "Big Cannon." Buchanan doubted Getumbe's innocence. To punish the chief, he ordered two hundred armed colonists to destroy Getumbe's village. Among the soldiers in Buchanan's army was Peyton Skipwith. He and the

others marched for three days through the forest until they reached the village, which was called Seuhn. There was an exchange of gunfire, and Skipwith received a leg wound that would take a year to heal. All that night and the next morning, the settler army burned the African village; then they began the long march home. Getumbe eluded capture, but following this show of strength, Buchanan easily persuaded the other inland chiefs to sign a treaty. Life in Millsburg and Caldwell was once more calm.

The upriver settlers interacted more closely with the Africans than their friends and relatives on the coast did. At first they did so from necessity: It took more labor to run their farms than the colonists could perform alone. Both recaptured and

Outside a Gola house. The man in Western dress appears to be literate and therefore probably is an American settler.

NATIVE BOYS from the jungles of AFRICA,

as they come into the LIBERIAN SETTLEMENTS with sword and spear

COPYRIGHT, 1880, by E.F.Hovey, 815 Arch Street, Philadelphia.

NATIVE AFRICAN BOYS

as they come to the Christian School House in LIBERIA, with ploughshare and pruning hook.

COPYRIGHT, 1880, BY E.F.HOVEY, 815 ARCH ST., PHILADELPHIA

These before-and-after pictures were intended to show the American public how exposure to Christianity and American culture benefited Liberia's native population. They also reflect common prejudice: The two Africans were called boys in the original captions, yet they clearly were young men.

native Africans worked on the upriver farms, and African children toiled alongside adults. Some colonists adopted African boys and girls. In return for their work, the children learned about settler culture by living with a family.

The children usually were adopted with their parents' approval. It was the custom among African peoples of the interior to exchange children as a sign of friendship and goodwill. The Africans had to nurse their pride, though, when the settlers declined to send some of their own children to live in African villages. There was no way that the Christian settlers would

The students and teachers of the St. Paul River Industrial School, circa 1900.

give away their children or let them grow up among "hea-thens."

To protect young wards, the colonial government required any child younger than eight who was living with an adoptive family to be bound by an apprenticeship contract. The contract detailed and limited the work that the child was to perform and the behavior that was expected of him or her. It also outlined the responsibilities of the employer, such as providing food, clothing, shelter, and education.

Several schools were soon built in the interior. In 1837, the Methodist Episcopal Church opened a vocational school near Millsburg that welcomed both settler and African children. This school taught trades and promoted understanding. Its teachers hoped that settler children would learn to treat their African classmates with greater kindness, and that the Africans would acquire "the language, the manners, the habits, and the charac-ter of a civilized people."

As the Africans working on upriver farms embraced Ameri-can culture, the colonists who employed them became more African in their ways. Some male settlers, for example, had more than one wife. It was not uncommon for an upriver man to have children with two women, one an American colonist and the other an African living in a native village. As a result, there are Liberians today who claim to be of native African heritage but who possess American settlers' surnames. In Monrovia and the other coastal towns, such mixing rarely occurred. In those places, "respectable" American settlers married only among themselves.

CHAPTER SIX

Progress

In 1840, about two thousand African-American immigrants made their homes in Liberia. Six hundred of their children had been born there. The population included farmers, bakers, and clerks as well as traders, carpenters, and housekeepers. Most educated people lived in Monrovia, the center of government and commerce. Monrovia was home to lawyers, doctors, ministers, and artisans such as Peyton Skipwith. The stonemason from Virginia had remarried, and his business had grown with the colony. He had trained his son Nash to work at his side, and he employed

several immigrant boys as apprentices and furnished them with food and shelter.

Eighteen years after Liberia's founding, life was easier and more comfortable for many of the pioneers. Fewer newcomers were dying from African fever. Once the settlers had observed that malaria attacks with less ferocity in the dry season, the American Colonization Society avoided sending people to Liberia after the rains began.

The people were healthier, but they were increasingly unhappy with their leadership. Some sent angry letters to the society's headquarters in Washington, D.C., complaining about the actions of the white governors. In 1834, there were allegations that Governor J. B. Pinney knowingly distributed spoiled cornmeal to the settlers; when people complained, he blamed a black storekeeper. In 1835, colonist John Lewis informed the American Colonization Society that Pinney was enriching his bank account by selling corned beef and pork at inflated prices.

The most serious accusation was leveled at Joseph Mechlin, who succeeded Jehudi Ashmun as governor. Settler Joseph Blake wrote that Mechlin "by criminal conversation decoyed my wife away" and raped her. Blake insisted that the light-skinned child his wife later bore was Mechlin's. (Mechlin had returned to the United States by the time Blake wrote his letter and was never charged with rape.)

The people thought that a black colony ought to have a black leader, and when governor "Big Cannon" Buchanan died on September 13, 1841, Joseph Jenkins Roberts took his place.

Roberts, the successful trader from Virginia, had served as lieutenant governor for three years.

Foreign nations had little respect for the colony or its black governor. Although Liberia claimed to control 240 miles of coastline, foreign merchants ignored the government's authority. These seagoing traders dropped anchor wherever they pleased to come ashore and do business with the native Africans. One British sea captain called Liberia's efforts to regulate trade and collect export duties "an offensive attempt to injure our commerce." The British wanted to know what gave a private organization like the American Colonization Society the right to make laws and demand taxes.

The colony depended on customs duties for most of its income, but it lacked the power to make European nations obey its laws. Roberts and other leading colonists understood that Liberia itself needed to become a nation. They put the matter to a vote, and in October 1846, the settlers elected to become Africa's first independent republic.

Unlike the American colonies in North America, which went to war in 1776 to gain their independence, Liberia separated from the American Colonization Society in 1847 without a struggle. The society's members had grown weary of supporting their African settlement and were glad to let it go. Since 1822, the society had been hiring ships to transport people and stocking those ships with food and supplies for the emigrants en route. The society had funded schools in Liberia as well as a courthouse and jail; it had paid for buildings, fortifications, roads, land, and gifts for African rulers. Donations never

"We were made a separate and distinct class and against us every avenue of improvement was effectually closed."

equaled expenses, and by the mid-1830s, the American Colonization Society was deeply in debt. Nevertheless, the members would continue to send African Americans to Liberia until the time of the American Civil War, and they would help to handle Liberia's business affairs until 1964, when the society was officially disbanded due to waning interest.

In 1847, in the middle of the rainy season, a group of elected delegates met in Monrovia to draw up a declaration of independence and a constitution for their new nation. The Liberian Declaration of Independence described the "grinding oppression" that had caused so many African Americans to leave the United States:

"In some parts of that country we were debarred from all rights and privileges of men—in other parts, public sentiment, more powerful than law, frowned us down. . . .

"We were made a separate and distinct class and against us every avenue of improvement was effectually closed. Strangers from other lands, of a color different from ours, were preferred before us. . . ."

The authors of the Declaration of Independence wrote, "In coming to the barbarous shores of Africa we indulged the pleasing hope that we would be permitted to exercise and improve those faculties which impart to man his dignity. . . ."

At the time of the declaration, Liberia included all settlements founded by the American Colonization Society and all the state settlements except Maryland in Liberia. The Maryland colony would not unite with the nation of Liberia until 1857.

Simon Greenleaf, a law professor at Harvard University,

helped to write Liberia's constitution. According to this document, Liberia was to have a government modeled on that of the United States, with a president (serving an initial eight-year term and subsequent four-year terms), a senate, a house of representatives, and a supreme court. The constitution outlawed slavery and guaranteed all citizens freedom of religion and freedom of the press. It granted the right to vote to adult male citizens who owned property. But whether everyone who lived in Liberia was entitled to the rights of citizenship was a tough question for that nation's founding fathers to resolve. The constitution of 1847 extended the rights of citizenship to all immi-

Monrovia resident Robert K. Griffin created this painting of the Liberian Senate around 1856.

LIBERIA

1847–1893

The Liberian flag adorns the cover of a pamphlet distributed at the World's Columbian Exposition, held in Chicago in 1893. The author of the pamphlet called Liberia "the happy home of thousands."

grants of African lineage who were twenty-one years of age and owned real estate, and to their descendants. In 1862, however, the Supreme Court of Liberia declared that the native people were subjects—not citizens—and that the constitution granted them civil rights but not political rights, such as the right to vote.

On August 24, 1847, a crowd of Americo-Liberians (as the settlers now called themselves) gathered in Monrovia, the capital, to watch as their nation's flag was raised for the first time. The flag was red, white, and blue, like that of the United States. Its eleven stripes—six red and five white—honored the eleven signers of the Liberian Declaration of Independence. Its upper left corner bore a single white star against a blue background, because Liberia was one state instead of many. When the ceremony ended, the people feasted on the foods of their nation and raised glasses of water to drink toasts.

Among the early settlers who lived to see Liberia become independent were several members of the Skipwith family. Peyton Skipwith lived in Monrovia until 1849, when, as his daughter Matilda wrote to John Hartwell Cocke, "he fell to sleep in Jesus Arms never more to have earthly communications with you all. . . ." Matilda Skipwith, who had come to Liberia as a nine-year-old child, married twice. Her first husband was named Richardson. After he died, she married a man named

There are no known photographs of the Skipwiths; only their letters survive. Matilda Skipwith Lomax wrote this letter to John Hartwell Cocke on May 19, 1852.

Lomax. She did sailors' laundry to help make ends meet, and she belonged to the Daughters of Temperance and the Sisters of Friendship. The date of her death is unknown.

Joseph Jenkins Roberts was elected Liberia's first president in October 1847. On January 3, 1848, he stood before the nation's senators and representatives to deliver his inaugural

Joseph Jenkins Roberts, first president of Liberia. After leaving office in 1856, Roberts became president of the newly founded Liberia College. He served again as the nation's president from 1872 until 1876.

address. "The time has been," he said, "when men . . . might have doubted the feasibility of establishing an independent Christian state on this coast, composed of, and conducted wholly by Coloured men,—but, fellow citizens, that time has passed, and I believe in my soul, that the permanency of the government of the Republic of Liberia is now fixed upon as firm a basis as human wisdom is capable of devising." He praised God, "that all-gracious Providence, who, by His unerring ways, has, with so few sufferings on our part . . . led us to this happy stage in our progress. . . ."

Immediately, Roberts worked to secure the coastline. He sailed to London, where he signed a treaty of friendship and commerce with the British government. He visited Queen Victoria on the royal yacht, and she presented Liberia with a warship and a transport vessel. Over the next few years, Liberia received formal recognition from most of the countries in western Europe, Haiti, and Brazil. Yet the United States refused to recognize Liberia as an independent nation, because powerful southern politicians did not want a black diplomat residing in Washington, D.C.

Another task for the Liberian government was to define the boundaries of the new nation. The legislators claimed all land between 4°41′ and 6°48′ north latitude and 8°8′ and 11°20′ west longitude. With an average width of 45 miles and a coastline stretching southeast from the Sewa River to the Grand Cess River, Liberia encompassed 12,830 square miles. The colony born on 4,200 acres ceded by King Peter in 1821 was now a

The president's mansion. In the twentieth century, this building served as the National Museum, housing native artifacts and antiques from Liberia's colonial period.

nation a little bit larger than Massachusetts and Connecticut combined, and it would continue to grow.

In 1857, the government of Liberia held its first National Fair to show off "the skill, industry and ingenuity of the citizens of this Republic. . . ." A Committee of Inspection was to award cash prizes for the best farm animals, produce, and handcrafts. For eight days in December, Monrovia's Government Square was jammed with people, cattle, turkeys, hogs, sacks of coffee and rice, bunches of bananas, furniture, and bolts of hand-woven cloth. Ninety-one people won prizes. James B. Yates, who lived alongside the St. Paul River, received three dollars for his outstanding four-month-old ram. Isaac C. Jackson of the town of Bexley won five dollars for growing a hundred pounds of ginger on a single hill, while a Mr. Leiper of Monrovia was

The Legation of the Netherlands, Broad Street, Monrovia. The Netherlands was one of the first nations to establish diplomatic relations with Liberia.

given one dollar for producing a small quantity of very fine ginger. Mrs. F. P. David of Monrovia received five dollars for sewing a splendid coat and matching pair of pantaloons.

The government that rewarded citizens for their industry at the National Fair soon faced a crisis. The United States was sending an enormous number of recaptured people to Liberia,

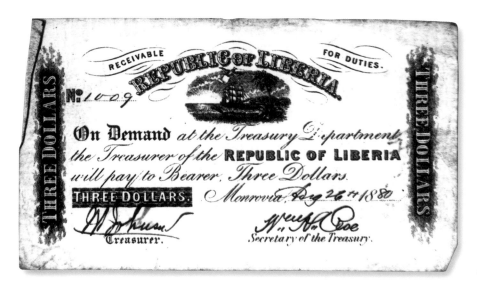

A Liberian three-dollar bill. Liberia modeled its dollars-and-cents monetary system on that of the United States.

more than the young nation could readily absorb. The recaptured population had begun to rise markedly in 1846, when the U.S. Navy brought to Liberia 756 people who had been rescued from the slave ship *Pons*. As in the past, many of the recaptureds were bound into apprenticeship. To spread the new arrivals throughout the country and prevent a large number from settling in Monrovia, the government paid upriver farmers fifty cents and Monrovians twenty-five cents for each recaptured African taken in. The government also provided each recaptured person with clothes and bedding, because the citizens could not afford to outfit so many people.

By 1860, more than 5,400 recaptureds had come. There were nearly as many recaptureds as Americo-Liberians, and the apprentice system could no longer take them all in. Christian missionaries gave shelter to large numbers of people, especially children. Many recaptured Africans lived at a Lutheran mission located beside the rapids of the St. Paul River, while twenty recaptured boys and girls attended a Presbyterian boarding school in the town of Harrisburg. Some recaptured people founded settlements of their own, which the Americo-Liberians called "Congo towns," and helped to populate the frontier.

In 1861, the *Liberia Herald* printed the words to a song that the recaptured Africans sang about life in their new land:

> *Here food and drink we find,*
> *And pity, too, is shown;*
> *Is not known,*
> *Is not known,*
> *The future is not known.*

"Some Fertile Country"

As the Americo-Liberians celebrated their independence and held fairs, people in the United States continued to debate the pros and cons of colonization. These arguments were part of a larger clamor about slavery. The abolitionists had grown in number and now called in a powerful voice for an end to the owning of slaves. "It is the duty of all men," said the abolitionist Elizur Wright, Jr., "to urge upon slaveholders immediate emancipation, so long as there is a slave. . . ."

Even the majority of northerners, who had hoped slavery

would gradually die out on its own, were having trouble staying silent. The issue that inspired them to speak out was the spread of slaveholding into the West. They were incensed that southerners wanted to bring slaves into new territories and states west of the Mississippi River. Congress tried to compromise, to pass laws that would prevent the rift between South and North from widening. One such trade-off, the Missouri Compromise of 1820, admitted Missouri and Maine to the Union, one as a slave state and the other free. It also outlawed slavery north of 36°30′ latitude.

The Fugitive Slave Law of 1850 permitted slave catchers to remove people from their homes by force.

Thirty years later, the Compromise of 1850 appeased the North by permitting California to enter the Union as a free state and outlawing the slave trade in the District of Columbia. As a concession to the South, it included a harsh Fugitive Slave Law, which provided for the return of runaway slaves to their masters, even to masters showing scanty proof of ownership. Under this law, anyone caught aiding an escapee was to be severely punished.

The new law and the threat that it posed to their freedom caused many blacks who had opposed emigration to change their minds. Augustus Washington, the earliest known black

Before emigrating to Liberia, Augustus Washington ran a thriving daguerreotype business on the top floor of the Kellogg Building in Hartford, Connecticut (the tall building at the left). Washington made many portraits of customers in the United States and in Liberia, but no photographs of him are known to exist.

A stirring speaker, Frederick Douglass appeared at many abolitionist rallies. Here he attends an 1850 antislavery meeting in a Cazenovia, New York, apple orchard. Douglass, in a white shirt and black coat, sits to the right of the table.

photographer in the United States, wrote in 1851 that if African Americans were "ever [to] find a home on earth for the development of their manhood and intellect it [would] first be in Liberia or some other part of Africa." Just ten years earlier, Washington had announced, "I abhor with intense hatred the motives, the scheme, and spirit of colonization." Washington closed his studio in 1853 and moved with his wife and two small children from Hartford, Connecticut, to Liberia.

Other prominent African Americans, including the physician and journalist Martin Delany, favored black resettlement in a section of West Africa that is now part of Nigeria. In 1859, Delany led an expedition to explore the Niger Delta as a place for colonization. The colony was never more than an idea, because Delany returned to the United States on the eve of the Civil War and devoted himself to emancipation rather than colonization. (During the war, he recruited soldiers for the Union Army, and on February 27, 1865, he was commissioned a major of the infantry.)

The most outspoken African American of the mid-nineteenth century remained firmly against emigration, however. Frederick Douglass called colonization the hateful, unchristian "twin-sister of slavery." The United States and not Africa, Douglass said, was the black American's native land. "He, if any one, has a right to the soil of this continent."

Douglass stated, "We want colored men, when colonizationists press upon them the propriety of emigrating to Liberia, or any where else, to give them this simple and decided answer: *We will not go!*"

In 1858, the Republicans of Illinois nominated Congressman Abraham Lincoln for the United States Senate. Debating his opponent, Democrat Steven Douglas, Lincoln said, "If all earthly power were given to me . . . My first impulse would be to free all the slaves and send them to Liberia. . . ." Lincoln thought that black and white Americans were so different, in both appearance and culture, that they never would live as equals in the United States. He admitted, though, that shipping to Africa the nearly 4 million people enslaved in the South would be impossible.

The number of slaves in the United States had increased markedly since 1830, and the number of free blacks was approaching 488,000. Forty-four percent of free blacks lived in the Southeast, mostly in cities and large towns. In cities such as Baltimore and Washington, they outnumbered the enslaved. Forty-six percent of free African Americans made their homes in the North, and the remainder had migrated west.

Lincoln lost the senate race, but his debates with Douglas gained him national recognition. In 1860, the American people elected him president of the United States. Although he had the support of many abolitionists, Lincoln did not share their intensity. He did feel that slavery was a moral evil, saying, "If slavery is not wrong, then nothing is wrong." But as long as the Constitution protected slavery and the nation was at peace, he was willing to let the hateful practice continue in states where it already existed.

Nevertheless, his victory so alarmed southern leaders that seven states—South Carolina, Florida, Alabama, Georgia,

Mississippi, Louisiana, and Texas—seceded. In February 1861, they formed a separate government. By April of that year, Virginia, Tennessee, Arkansas, and North Carolina had also seceded and become part of the new southern nation, the Confederate States of America. On April 12, 1861, the Confederates attacked Fort Sumter, the U.S. military post in the harbor of Charleston, South Carolina. That event marked the start of the American Civil War.

As commander in chief in this war to reunite the nation, Lincoln held fast to his belief that deportation of blacks was a way to solve the racial problems of the United States. In the spring of 1862, he introduced a bill in Congress to make one hundred thousand dollars of federal funds available for relocating African Americans outside U.S. borders. He insisted, though, that any African Americans who might leave the United States at government expense would do so of their own free will. Lincoln signed the bill into law on April 16. Two months later, Congress set aside another five hundred thousand dollars for the deportation of blacks living in sections of the South that came under Union military control.

As northern forces pressed southward, thousands of slaves escaped from plantations and sought their protection. Union officers employed many of the men to build bridges, repair railroad tracks, and do other work that aided the war effort. And in May 1862, ex-slaves were trained as soldiers for the first time. (Eventually, about 186,000 African Americans from the South and the North would fight for the Union in the Civil War; 38,000 of them would die from battlefield wounds or disease.)

The military employed only a fraction of the former slaves, and Union generals were at a loss about what to do with the rest. They herded people into camps at places like Grand Junction, Tennessee; De Soto, Louisiana; and Arlington, Virginia, which had been the home of Confederate general Robert E. Lee. Life in these camps was grim. Ragged children, women, and old men crowded together in tents pitched on muddy ground, and there was never enough food. Every day camp residents died of starvation and disease. In the summer of 1863, a witness at the Young's Point, Louisiana, camp saw "thousands of people dying without well ones enough to inter the dead."

On August 14, 1862, Lincoln met with five African-American ministers at the White House to express his thoughts on colonization. He told the men, "I think your race suffer very greatly, many of them by living among us, while ours suffer from your presence. In a word we suffer on each side. If this is admitted, it affords a reason at least why we should be separated." The Reverend Edwin Thomas, chairman of the African-American delegation, told the president that the men would discuss the matter of colonization and let him know their thoughts, but whether they ever responded is unknown.

Some of Lincoln's advisers openly objected to the colonization plan. Commenting on Lincoln's words to the African-American ministers, Treasury Secretary Salmon P. Chase said, "How much better would be a manly protest against prejudice against color!—and a wise effort to give freedmen homes in America!"

Escaped slaves arrive in a Union Army camp in Virginia. The soldiers called these refugees from slavery "contrabands."

Such outcries failed to persuade Lincoln, who now hoped to found a new African-American colony somewhere in the Western Hemisphere. At first, he selected a site in Panama called Chiriqui. He had been told that this region held rich coal reserves, and he thought that the colonists could earn a good living as miners. Chiriqui's tropical climate was another plus. At that time, many whites thought that blacks' bodies were adapted for survival in hot, humid conditions such as those in West Africa. (Even as late as 1909, the public was amazed that the African-American explorer Matthew Henson could stay alive at the North Pole.)

Lincoln abandoned the Chiriqui project in October 1862, when Nicaragua, Honduras, and Costa Rica lodged an official protest with the United States government. Those nations did not want a U.S. colony for a neighbor, especially one populated by black immigrants who were unwelcome in the land of their birth. A diplomat representing the three nations hinted that they were ready to use military force to repel an invasion of African-American colonists.

The second place chosen for colonization was Île à Vache, a small island located about ninety miles southwest of Port au Prince, the capital of Haiti. An American adventurer named Bernard Kock had leased the island from the Haitian government. In a meeting with the president, Kock described Île à Vache as a place of great beauty. Its forests held valuable timber, he said, and its soil and climate were ideal for raising sugar, coffee, and cotton. Kock offered to settle five thousand African Americans on Île à Vache at a cost to the government of fifty dollars each. He promised to furnish the settlers with food, medical care, comfortable housing, farmland, churches, and schools. Then, secretly, Kock devised a scheme with northern investors to reap large profits from the settlers' toil. Lincoln learned about this second agreement, and he canceled the contract with Kock.

A group of American businessmen took over the lease on Île à Vache and signed their own contract with the government on April 6, 1863. Days later, 453 willing settlers set sail for the Caribbean island, but the venture soon proved disastrous. Thirty-eight emigrants died of smallpox aboard ship. The others reached their destination only to find that no houses had been built for them. Weakened by malaria, they lacked the energy needed to coax crops from the island's poor soil. When word reached Washington that eighty-five settlers had died of hunger, thirst, and disease, the government chartered a ship to bring the survivors home. Congress promptly withdrew all funds for black resettlement.

As the government experimented with colonization, events occurred that gave African Americans hope for a better life in the United States. For one thing, northern missionaries and teachers were traveling to occupied sections of the South to prepare black children and adults for lives as free Americans. For another, Congress abolished slavery in the District of Columbia in April 1862. Two months later, President Lincoln signed an executive order making it illegal to own slaves in western territories. Also in 1862, the United States formally recognized the governments of Liberia and Haiti, another nation established by black former slaves.

In the Emancipation Proclamation, a document that took effect January 1, 1863, Lincoln declared that all people enslaved in places controlled by the Confederacy would be "thenceforward, and forever free." The proclamation made no real difference in the lives of Confederate slaves, because their owners were not about to follow orders from the president of the United States, but this historic document let people south and north know that the United States was now fighting the Civil War to free the slaves.

And the United States was winning. By early 1865, the Con-

"If slavery is not wrong, then nothing is wrong."

"Emancipation," a statue by Thomas Ball. The Emancipation Proclamation inspired Ball to sculpt Lincoln uplifting an enslaved African American.

federacy was a charred and plundered nation. Southern cities fell to the northern armies in quick succession: Mobile, Selma, and Montgomery in Alabama, then Petersburg and Richmond, the Confederate capital, in Virginia. On April 9, 1865, Robert E. Lee surrendered to Union general Ulysses S. Grant at Appomattox Courthouse, Virginia. The Confederate forces that remained in the field quickly broke up, and the Civil War was over. Slavery in the United States had become a part of history.

Whether Lincoln ever changed his mind about the worthiness of deporting blacks may never be known. On July 1, 1864, his private secretary, John Hays, wrote, "I am glad the President has sloughed off that idea of colonization." But Hays may have been an unreliable witness. He had always strongly opposed colonization himself, calling it "a hideous & barbarous humbug. . . ."

Union general Benjamin F. Butler claimed that with victory upon him, Lincoln was still searching for a way to resettle African Americans in a land of their own. Butler reported that Lincoln said in February 1865, "I can hardly believe that the South and North can live in peace unless we get rid of the Negroes. . . . I believe that it would be better to export them all

President Lincoln shows Sojourner Truth a Bible presented to him by the African Americans of Baltimore. The famous abolitionist and advocate of women's rights visited the White House on October 29, 1864.

to some fertile country with a good climate, which they could have to themselves." No one can confirm the truth of Butler's account, because no one else heard Lincoln say those words.

Butler said that he explained what Lincoln already knew, that such a scheme would never work. Even if every available ship were employed full-time to carry emigrants to a nearby island, the number of black babies born in the United States would soon outnumber the people who had been deported.

CHAPTER EIGHT

"The Beclouded Sun"

On January 7, 1856, a group of prominent Americo-Liberians sat down to a sumptuous banquet in Government Square, Monrovia. They had come to honor Stephen Allen Benson, the second president of Liberia, who had been inaugurated that day.

The outgoing president, Joseph Jenkins Roberts, spoke to the gathering about his country's past and present. "Liberia, in her progress, has had her seasons of sunshine, and of dark portentous clouds. . . . She has had her seasons of peace and war," he said. "But, fellow-citizens, we have passed triumphantly through

them all, and today we behold Liberia no longer a doubtful experiment—but, in verity and truth, a reality."

When it was his turn to speak, President Benson talked about the time to come. He predicted "a glorious future for Liberia, a future whose glory will exceed the present in brilliancy, far more than the clear noonday does the beclouded morning sun."

Roberts, Benson, and their fellow citizens were certain that the years of struggling were over. Liberia was a success, a nation among nations. They expected their country to grow steadily with immigration from North America, and when the American Civil War began, they made ready to welcome the boatloads of refugees that were bound to arrive from the United States. Between 1861 and 1865, as the war raged, however, fewer than two hundred African Americans moved to Liberia. The immigration rate rose between 1865 and 1868, but not by much. In 1865, Liberia was happy to receive 346 people from Barbados. These immigrants sought an escape from poverty, which was widespread in the British island colony, and the chance to live in a free black nation.

So much was happening in the United States immediately after the Civil War that few black Americans had time to think about moving overseas. It was a stirring, hopeful time for the former slaves. The Thirteenth Amendment to the Constitution, which abolished slavery throughout the United States, was ratified eight months after the war ended, in December 1865. Millions were discovering how it felt to be free, to live together as families without fear of separation. The former slaves were at liberty to worship whenever and wherever they chose, to move from one place to another, and to go to school.

Many blacks valued education highly, believing it would open doors to opportunity. "I could hardly believe my eyes—looking at my own little ones carrying their books under their arms," remarked Ambrose Headen, an ex-slave, in 1866. "I rubbed my eyes and said, 'Ambrose, you must be dreaming.'" Northern missionaries and the Freedmen's Bureau, a government agency, were opening schools for African Americans throughout the South. In 1870, the Freedmen's Bureau operated 4,329 schools where 247,333 children and adults were learning to read and write. Fisk University in Nashville, Tennessee, Howard University in Washington, D.C., and other black colleges and universities were also established in the decades following the Civil War.

African Americans looked forward to being active in commerce and politics, although southern whites sought ways to prevent their success. One by one, the southern states passed Black Codes, which were laws that restricted the activities of African Americans. These codes varied from state to state, but they had several features in common. For example, they all spelled out where African Americans could rent or buy property. They also included tough vagrancy laws that forced African Americans into low-paying jobs. In most southern states, blacks could be jailed or sentenced to forced labor unless they could prove that they were employed; many had no option but to hire themselves out to white planters for meager wages. "This is not the condition of really free men," protested African

Stephen Allen Benson, Liberia's second president.

Americans in the Sea Islands of South Carolina, to no avail. Louisiana's Black Code required African-American farm hands to get the boss's permission before leaving the fields, as if they were still enslaved.

Northerners in Congress were so concerned about the treatment of blacks in the states of the former Confederacy that they overrode a veto by President Andrew Johnson to pass into law the Civil Rights Act of 1866. This law defined the rights of citizens and nullified the Black Codes. Again overriding a presidential veto, Congress passed the Reconstruction Act of 1867, which placed most of the South under military control and pro-

A freedmen's school in Memphis, Tennessee, 1866.

tected the right of African-American men to vote. (American women of all races would not be permitted to vote until 1920.)

Two amendments to the Constitution further secured the rights protected under these laws. The Fourteenth Amendment, which extended the full rights of citizenship to the former slaves and guaranteed equal protection under the law, was ratified in 1868. In February 1870, a majority of states approved the Fifteenth Amendment, which barred the federal and state governments from denying anyone the right to vote because of "race, color, or previous condition of servitude."

Throughout the South, African Americans registered to vote, ran for office, and won elections. There were 87 black representatives and 40 whites in the first legislature elected in South Carolina after the Civil War, in 1868. In Mississippi, African Americans won 55 of the 115 seats in the state House in 1873, and 9 of the 37 seats in the state Senate. Mississippi had a black lieutenant governor in 1873, and a black superintendent of education. At the state and community level, African-American politicians made sure that blacks and whites were taxed fairly and benefited equally from such tax-supported programs as road building and relief for the poor. They helped to create public-school systems, hospitals, and orphanages.

Blacks also represented their states in Washington, D.C. The first to do so was Hiram Revels, who was elected to the U.S. Senate by the Mississippi legislature in January 1870. (State legislatures chose all U.S. senators until 1913, when the Seventeenth Amendment to the Constitution provided for the election of senators by popular vote.) Blanche Kelso Bruce of Missis-

"Today we behold Liberia no longer a doubtful experiment—but, in verity and truth, a reality."

Many African Americans, young and old, continued to do agricultural work after the Civil War. These Floridians are picking cotton.

sippi, elected in 1875, was the first African American to serve a complete senate term, and he was the only one to do so until the middle of the twentieth century.

Although African Americans gained some political power in the South, whites were always in control. Most southern whites agreed with Governor Benjamin G. Humphreys of Mississippi, who said in 1865, "Ours is, and it ever shall be, a government of white men." Even in 1868, when so many blacks were elected to the state legislature in South Carolina, most of the state's senators were white, and so was the governor. Throughout the South, black legislators were unable to stop whites from using every conceivable method to force African Americans back into a second-class role.

Beginning in 1875, southern states and cities enacted the

An aging man casts his very first vote on Election Day 1867.

"Jim Crow" laws, which separated society along racial lines. These laws called for separate seating for blacks and whites on streetcars as well as separate schools, train cars, and railway waiting rooms. Blacks were banished from restaurants, hotels, and other businesses that served whites.

Southern white legislators also found ways to sidestep the Fifteenth Amendment to make it nearly impossible for African Americans to vote. Between 1877 and 1889, the southern states began to charge a fee for voting, called a poll tax, knowing that few black voters could afford to pay it. Southern states also commonly insisted that voters pass tough literacy tests that were rigged in favor of whites. Maryland, a former slave state that had remained loyal to the union, kept most African Americans from having a voice in elections by requiring all voters to own property.

The Ku Klux Klan, Knights of the White Camelia, and other white-supremacist groups used fear and violence to block African Americans from voting, going to school, or making any kind of progress. They made threats, burned blacks' houses and barns, and destroyed their crops. Blacks who challenged white authority risked beating, whipping, or lynching at the hands of these hate groups. One man was whipped for failing to tip his hat while passing a white man on the street. A congressional committee investigating these atrocities concluded that the Ku Klux Klan was operating "a carnival of murders, intimidation, and violence of all kinds." But attempts by the federal government to punish the terrorists failed, because few whites were willing to give evidence against them and white juries refused to convict them. (Only voters sat on juries, so it was rare for an African American to help decide a defendant's innocence or guilt.)

By the late 1870s, emigration once more appealed to many blacks who were fed up with their treatment in American society. "I would make Africa a place of refuge, because I see no other shelter from the stormy blast, from the red tide of persecution, from the horrors of American prejudice," cried the most vocal supporter of emigration, Bishop Henry McNeal Turner of the African Methodist Episcopal Church. Turner used his pulpit to warn blacks that what had happened to Native Americans at the hands of whites could also happen to them. At the very least, blacks in the United States would be forever barred from accomplishing all that they might do. "There is no more doubt in my mind that we have ultimately to return to Africa than there is of the existence of God," said the devout bishop, who, ironically, would remain a lifelong resident of the United States.

On March 21, 1878, Turner spoke at an outdoor religious service held in Charleston, South Carolina, to consecrate the *Azor*, a ship intended to carry people to Liberia. The *Azor*, Turner told his audience of five thousand, "was not only to bear a load of humanity, but to take back the culture, education, and

A member of the Ku Klux Klan from Tennessee, photographed around 1868. More than fifty years later, in the 1920s, the Klan adopted the white robes that became their trademark.

The Azor *in Charleston Harbor, March 21, 1878.*

religion acquired here." The passengers were going to spread the word of God, Turner said, never stopping "until the blaze of Gospel truth should glitter over the whole broad African continent."

With the American Colonization Society supporting schools and religious missionaries in its former colony, rather than emigration, private firms transported most Liberia-bound travelers after the Civil War. The *Azor* belonged to the Liberian Exodus Joint Stock Steamship Company, a firm founded by well-to-do Charleston blacks to transport people to Africa. It set sail on April 21, 1878, beginning an ocean crossing that was nearly as dismal as the voyage of the *Elizabeth* in 1820. Twenty-three of the 206 people making the journey became sick and died. The supply of fresh water ran out, and the dirty, almost inedible food had to be carefully rationed. Instead of earning a profit for the steamship company, the voyage resulted in debt. The *Azor* made no more trips to Liberia, and in November 1879, it was sold.

Edward Wilmot Blyden, one of nineteenth-century Liberia's finest minds.

In 1890, one of Liberia's leading citizens, Edward Wilmot Blyden, came to the United States to convince American blacks to settle in Africa. Born in St. Thomas, Virgin Islands, in 1832, Blyden had lived in Venezuela and the United States before arriving in Liberia in 1850. He had edited the *Liberia Herald* and helped to found Liberia College, where he taught classics. Blyden traveled through the South and North giving speeches in praise of his adopted country. He also endorsed a bill that had been introduced in the U.S. Congress by Senator Matthew Butler of South Carolina.

The Butler Bill called for the federal government to give financial aid to southern blacks wishing to become citizens of other countries. Butler had drafted the bill because he had the interests of whites rather than blacks at heart: He wanted to remove African Americans from the southern states to keep them from voting there.

Although there were blacks and whites who supported the bill, most Americans opposed it. Many northerners called it immoral to send American citizens away from their homeland, while southern planters worried about losing their cheap black labor. The Butler Bill failed to receive enough votes to become law.

The Americo-Liberians had counted on an exodus from the United States to build their society and economy. As the nineteenth century came to an end, they understood that their future would not be as bright as President Stephen Allen Benson had predicted, and that there would be no great flight to Africa. "We are keeping these lands, we say, for our brethren in America," concluded Edward Wilmot Blyden. "But they are not willing to come, and they will not be ready to come for the next hundred years."

American blacks remained curious about their brothers and sisters across the ocean, however, and about life in the still-young country of Liberia. In 1920, the African-American educator and writer Benjamin Brawley spent six months in Liberia studying its society and schools. He was disappointed to report that the nation lacked railroads, streetcars, and public education. Religious and charitable groups operated all the schools. Also, there were too few jobs available for all the young men seeking employment. Brawley noted that although several found work in stores or in the customs house, some of the most promising youths "come to America to be educated and not always do they return. . . .

"The comparative isolation of the Republic moreover, and

the general stress of living conditions have together given to the everyday life an undue seriousness of tone with a rather excessive emphasis on the church, on politics, and on secret societies," Brawley continued. He observed that in such a somber atmosphere girls and boys too early took on the worries of grown women and men. He wrote, "[F]or them especially one might wish to see a little more wholesome outdoor amusement."

African Americans still nurtured dreams of equality in the first decades of the twentieth century, but when some 1.5 million blacks left the rural South in search of a better life, they went to the industrial cities of the North, and not to Liberia. They left seeking jobs in factories, better schools for their children, and escape from the heavy hand of Jim Crow. They found jobs, but always at low pay and requiring little skill; schools that were segregated by tradition rather than by law; and landlords who charged them high rent for crowded housing in rundown neighborhoods. The quest for racial equality in the United States would continue into the twenty-first century.

Liberia, Troubled Land

At the start of the twenty-first century, Liberia is a war-torn country. Many of its citizens live in poverty, and the crime rate is high. Even in Monrovia, streets are in poor condition, there are no working traffic lights, and hospitals lack the necessary equipment and medicine to treat the ill. On May 31, 2001, the U.S. State Department officially warned Americans against traveling in Liberia because of the potential that exists there for violence.

Without the hoped-for immigration from the United States, Liberia failed to prosper. By the late nineteenth century, the

sugar and coffee industries were in decline. Cuba had become the world's top sugar producer, and the United States preferred to import its sugar from that nearby island than from far-off Liberia. At the same time, Brazil had captured a large share of the world's coffee market. Liberia's leaders therefore turned to foreign countries for financial help. In 1871, the government accepted a loan from a British bank at a high rate of interest, and repaying the debt nearly destroyed the national economy.

The Liberians also had trouble protecting their borders. During the 1880s, European powers were greedily carving up Africa into colonies. The empire builders included Great Britain, France, Germany, Belgium, Italy, and Portugal.

Seen from a distance in this 1986 photograph, Monrovia looks like a peaceful, thriving city.

Because rivalry among these nations was intense, and because they often argued about the boundaries of their colonies, there was a constant threat of war. In November 1884, delegates from the United States and the European nations met in Berlin to begin a year-long conference at which the Europeans would decide how to divide Africa and how to live together on that continent without fighting. The delegates drew up rules, for example, for navigation on the Congo and Niger Rivers, two important routes to the African interior.

The delegates agreed to keep their hands off Liberia and Ethiopia, two independent nations, but otherwise, they paid no attention to the wishes of the African people. They did not even invite any Africans to take part in the conference.

The Berlin agreements failed to prevent France and Great Britain from claiming portions of Liberia. In 1885, Liberia was forced to give up land west of the Mano River to its northwestern neighbor, the British colony Sierra Leone. In 1892, French military forces occupied land in southeast Liberia, east of the Cavalla River. Liberia's army was too weak to defend the territory, which became part of the new French colony Côte d'Ivoire (Ivory Coast). Finally, in 1911, Liberia ceded its holdings northeast of the Makona River to the French. What remained was a nation 43,000 square miles in area, just a little bit larger than Tennessee.

Despite these losses, Liberians were optimistic in 1927, when their leaders leased a million acres to the Firestone Tire and Rubber Corporation in exchange for the company's help in securing a five-million-dollar loan from the United States. Fire-

stone developed the world's largest rubber plantation on the land, but because the company processed its rubber and manufactured tires outside Liberia, the Liberians realized little profit from the venture. They also lost a portion of their country's natural beauty, because Firestone felled jungle trees and burned brush to clear the land for planting, destroying many animals' homes in the process.

A native African worker collects rubber fluid, or latex, on a Firestone plantation in 1947. Rubber trees must be five years old before their latex can be harvested.

Still, there was again reason to be hopeful in 1944, when William V. S. Tubman was elected president. Tubman promised to "strive with all my might to agglutinate and unify our population." He belonged to the True Whig Party, an elite Americo-Liberian political body that had controlled the government since 1869. Nevertheless, during his seven terms in office, he did

With Firestone came modernization. Monrovia gained electricity, chain stores, movie theaters, and automobiles. Before the rubber company arrived, the president was the only Liberian who owned a car. This photograph is from the first half of the twentieth century.

more than any other president to bring the native and Americo-Liberian populations closer together. In 1946, under his leadership, the native Liberians gained the right to vote and run for office. Tubman was still president in 1964, when the native people of the hinterlands were first represented in the national legislature. Most people of native heritage actually took little part in the political life of their nation, however. Although English was—and remains—Liberia's official language, nearly all the indigenous people spoke only African tongues.

The Liberians enjoyed peace and stability during Tubman's presidency, which occurred at a time when civil wars and political crises caused turmoil in much of Africa; but law and order came at a price. Tubman kept such strict control over government operations that he insisted on signing any check drawn on the national treasury for more than twenty-five dollars. He used police and intelligence organizations to browbeat his enemies, both real and imagined. Freedom of speech, freedom of the press, and freedom of assembly all suffered under Tubman's rule, but his friends prospered. By 1971, when Tubman died in office, two percent of Americo-Liberians controlled six tenths of the nation's wealth. This small minority grew even richer in the years ahead, while most Liberians stayed poor.

The next president, William R. Tolbert, Jr., who took office in 1971, cared more about increasing his family's power and affluence than about serving the people he led. He made one of his brothers minister of finance, while another was president of the senate. His two daughters held important jobs in the Ministry of Education.

"There are still Liberians who have not given up hope."

LEFT: *Native African boys make bricks that will be used to build a school for their village. This photograph was taken in 1956; before that year, many villages were without schools.*

RIGHT: *President Tubman (center, in glasses) prepares to step out with other dignitaries in this photograph from 1964.*

During Tolbert's presidency, the average Liberian worker earned seventy dollars a month. Most people worked in agriculture, mining, or manufacturing, doing unskilled labor that offered no chance for advancement. With nearly one fourth of the work force unemployed, the jobless rate equaled that of the United States in 1932, at the height of the Great Depression. People stretched every dollar to buy the things they needed, and prices rose sharply. In April 1979, a steep increase in the price of rice, the staple food of most Liberians, led to rioting.

Conditions worsened, and on April 12, 1980, seventeen noncommissioned officers of the Liberian Army overthrew the government that had been in operation since 1847 and assassinated President Tolbert. "The unemployment situation was so bad that there were more people looking for work than employed," stated the twenty-eight-year-old coup leader, Samuel Kanyon Doe, who was of native African descent. "Most of the people cannot afford $40 to buy a bag of rice. . . . The health situation is so terrible that nearly one out of every five newly born babies dies before reaching the age of one." Doe's soldiers publicly executed thirteen senior government officials and leaders of the True Whig Party.

U.S. Secretary of State Henry Kissinger, visiting Liberia in May 1976, greets President Tolbert. Kissinger was distressed by the poverty that he saw in Liberia.

Samuel K. Doe brought the African majority to power, but instead of solving Liberia's social problems, he instituted a reign of terror. People said that his initials stood for "steal, kill, and destroy." His forces arrested, jailed, and tortured Americo-Liberians, often for no reason. The executions continued, both in public and behind prison walls. The victims included not just Americo-Liberians but also some of Doe's comrades-in-arms, whom he accused of plotting to overthrow the military government.

Liberia adopted a new constitution on July 3, 1985, and in October 1985, Doe was elected president in a rigged vote. The following month, General Thomas Quiwonkpa, a one-time ally

Samuel K. Doe delivers a speech in Monrovia on April 12, 1981, the first anniversary of his successful coup.

of Doe's, led an unsuccessful attempt to force the new president out of office. Doe had Quiwonkpa put to death and his body displayed for all Liberians to see. Trusting no one now, Doe ordered the deaths of three thousand men, women, and children and the destruction of houses and property.

One of Quiwonkpa's conspirators, the Americo-Liberian Charles Taylor, escaped to Sierra Leone. Taylor returned to Liberia with a rebel army on Christmas Eve 1989 and brought down the dictatorship of President Doe. Liberia was plunged into a complicated and bloody civil war in which various native ethnic groups and the Americo-Liberians fought to gain control of the nation. Taylor's rebel forces publicly executed President Doe and paraded his body through the streets of Monrovia.

In 1995, the Economic Community of West African States (ECOWAS) brought the warring factions together and negotiated a peace treaty. (ECOWAS is an alliance of fifteen nations, including Liberia, that promotes economic cooperation in West Africa.) A newly formed Interim State Council prepared to hold national elections. By the time Charles Taylor was elected president in 1997 and the civil war was thought to be over, tens of thousands of Liberians had lost their lives.

Taylor demonstrated no more ability to lead a country than his predecessor had. As president, he did almost nothing to rebuild the utilities, roads, and communications systems that had been destroyed during nearly eight years of civil war. People who had been forced by the battles to flee their homes received very little government aid. In addition, the turmoil had prompted many businesses to pack up and leave the country.

Charles Taylor arrives at a polling place to cast his vote in the presidential election of July 19, 1997.

Then, in July 2000, rebel forces launched an attack against Taylor's regime, and the fighting resumed. World leaders were so alarmed that in March 2001 the United Nations placed Liberia under a strict arms embargo. Members of the U.N. were prohibited from selling any type of weapon or military vehicle or equipment to the Liberians. Yet the fighting went on.

Thousands of refugees fled to Côte d'Ivoire, telling of attacks on civilians by both the well-armed rebels and the government forces, and of killings, rapes, and torture. Nearly all the displaced people were women, children, and old men. "We are afraid and suffering too much," said one refugee, a thirty-year-old mother of two, in August 2001. "People are afraid of the dissidents and afraid of the government. They knock on the door in the daytime, to say they need manpower to fight, and the men disappear."

The plan to create a home in Africa for black Americans originated with white men who wished to rid the United States of its free black population. The colony that resulted from that plan, Liberia, promised freedom and opportunity to farmers, traders, and artisans, as well as to families like the Skipwiths. The settlers built Liberia into an independent nation governed by blacks, the first republic in Africa. Throughout the nineteenth century, Liberia beckoned to enslaved Americans and their descendants, offering them a home.

For a number of reasons, Liberia never became the shining star that its settlers envisioned. Too few Americans answered its call, and those who did set themselves apart from the native Africans. As a result, Liberia is one of several troubled spots throughout the world—places such as Northern Ireland and

May 5, 1996: At the port of Monrovia, where optimistic immigrants once came ashore, desperate refugees crowd aboard a freighter bound for Ghana and Nigeria.

Soldiers of a native African faction hostile to Charles Taylor move into the deserted streets of downtown Monrovia.

Israel—where people from different cultural or religious backgrounds have been unable to live together in peace. For more than a century, the Americo-Liberians held complete power and excluded the native population from decision making. The native people had fewer opportunities for jobs or social advancement than the Americo-Liberians did, and they earned lower wages. Inequality bred resentment, which led to violence.

More natives might have found a place in society if Liberia had built a thriving economy, but for years it was a huge task just to safeguard the nation's independence, and its leaders had no time to plan. Throughout the nineteenth century, there were hostilities between the settler and native populations that needed to be resolved. Foreign powers were encroaching upon Liberian territory, and they needed to be appeased. Also, debts to Great Britain and other nations crippled the Liberian economy.

Poverty in Liberia has more recent causes as well. For example, the civil wars that began in the 1980s have increased the number of households headed by widows. As these women and their children are left to fend for themselves, they grow poorer.

Whether it is possible for this country in crisis to rescue itself remains to be seen. Liberia must achieve peace before economic recovery and development can take place, and peace can take root only if people are willing to judge others according to their individual merits rather than their heritage.

Many Liberians love their country despite its painful past and violent present, and this is cause for optimism. "There are still Liberians who have not given up hope," one writer among them has stated. "They are willing and ready to pick up the pieces and mend the wounds."

Cape Palmas, circa 1840.

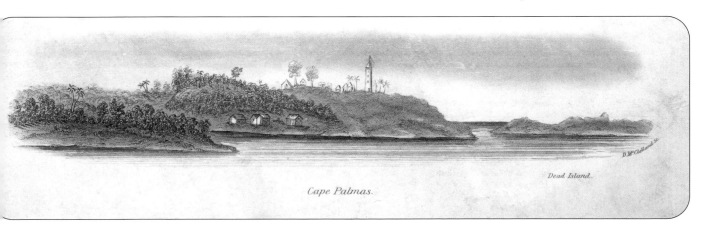

Cape Palmas.

Dead Island.

D.McClelland Sc

"Please Remember Me..."

A PORTRAIT GALLERY OF
NINETEENTH-CENTURY
LIBERIANS

(PHOTOGRAPH BY AUGUSTUS WASHINGTON)

Urias Africanus McGill, circa 1854.

(PHOTOGRAPH BY AUGUSTUS WASHINGTON)

*An unidentified woman
of the McGill family, circa 1855.*

(PHOTOGRAPH BY AUGUSTUS WASHINGTON)

*Jane Waring Roberts, wife of
Joseph Jenkins Roberts, circa 1851–1860.*

*Chancy Brown, sergeant-at-arms of the
Liberian Senate, circa 1856–1860.*

Two unidentified young men, circa 1840–1860.

Aunt Martha Rix,
nineteenth-century settler.

C. T. O. King, mayor of Monrovia,
circa 1895.

A Mandinka warrior, circa 1900.

General Robert A. Sherman
of the Liberian Army, circa 1895.

The wife of Joseph James Cheeseman,
president of Liberia from 1892 until 1896.

Sabro, a Vai prince, circa 1895.

The Liberian Senate, circa 1895.

OPPOSITE TOP: *The Episcopal bishop and clergy, circa 1895.*
OPPOSITE BOTTOM: *The faculty and scholars of Liberia College, circa 1893.*

Miss Jennie G. Sharp's School, located on the St. Paul River, 1893.

Group of Kru boys, circa 1900.

Liberia is a small country on the west coast of Africa.

AFRICA

LIBERIA

Monrovia

SOUTH
ATLANTIC
OCEAN

*A number of Liberia's early settlements were
established near the St. Paul River.*

St. Paul River

Millsburg ■ ■ Harrisburg

■ Caldwell

Stockton Creek

■ New Georgia

Mesurado River

Monrovia ★
CAPE
MESURADO

LIBERIA

ATLANTIC
OCEAN

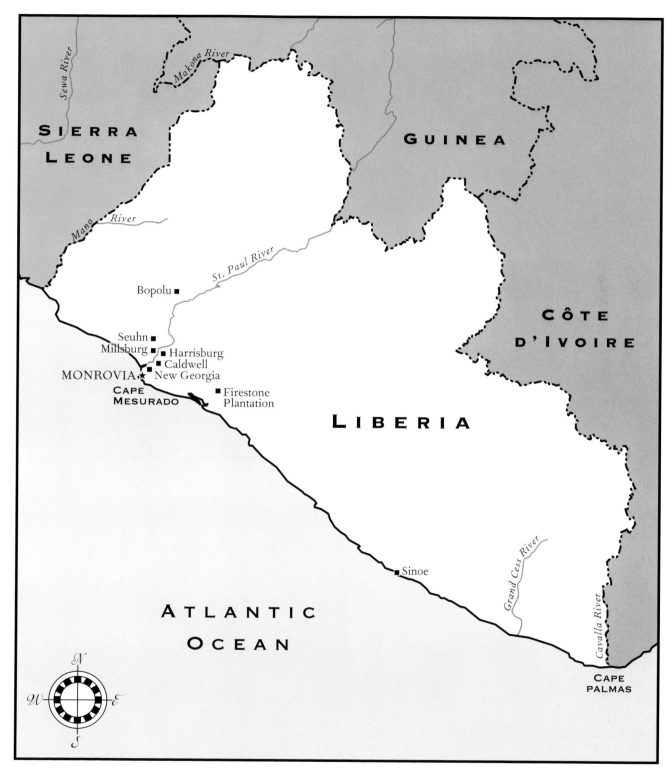

This map of Liberia shows the country's present-day borders.

A Note on the Photographs

The Liberian exhibit at the World's Columbian Exhibition. Visitors saw samples of native handcrafts and Liberian crops as well as birds' nests, the skins and heads of exotic animals, antelope horns, and hippopotamus tusks.

Liberia was founded in 1822, four years before Joseph Niepce made the world's first photograph, in France. Although by the 1840s photography was gaining popularity in Europe and the United States, it was late in coming to Liberia. For that reason, most of the photographs in this book are from the late nineteenth century. Some were made as souvenirs to be sold at the World's Columbian Exposition, a world's fair held in Chicago in 1893. Many are published here for the first time.

ENDNOTES

All cited books and articles are listed in the bibliography.

EPIGRAPH

Wilson, "Come hither, son of Afric . . ." is from "Liberia, Happy Land," in *Liberian Writing*, p. 16

CHAPTER ONE
"THESE FREE, SUNNY SHORES"

p. 4   "Little boys, and girls, too . . ." and "scoldings and beatings . . ." are from Jones, p. 8.

p. 6   "The quickness and luxuriance of the vegetation . . ." is from Alexander, p. 26.

p. 9   Matilda Skipwith, "I hope to see the day . . ." is quoted in Miller, p. 119.

p. 9   "I would rather, if need be . . ." is quoted in Shumard, p. 18.

CHAPTER TWO
"BEYOND THE REACH OF MIXTURE"

p. 11   Jefferson, "Nothing is more certainly written . . ." is quoted in Brodie, p. 441.

p. 11   Jefferson, "inferior to the whites . . ." and "beyond the reach of mixture" are from Jefferson, p. 139.

p. 12   Cuffe, "As I am of the African race . . ." is quoted in Harris, pp. 38–39.

p. 13	Cuffe, "My hope is in a coming day" is quoted in Sherwood, "Paul Cuffe," p. 390.
p. 15	Caldwell, "They can never enjoy equality . . ." is quoted in Sherwood, "Formation," p. 222.
p. 16	"men of virtue, piety, and reflection" is quoted in Sherwood, "Formation," p. 219.
p. 17	"peace on earth and good will to man," is quoted in Sherwood, "Formation," p. 223.
p. 18	Allen and Forten, "Humane and Benevolent Inhabitants . . ." and "outrage, having no other object . . ." are quoted in Franklin and Moss, p. 154.
p. 18	Walker, "America is more our country . . ." is from Walker, p. 21.

CHAPTER THREE
DIVINE PROVIDENCE

p. 19	"beyond the limits . . ." is quoted in Huberich, p. 68.
p. 22	Coker, "God moves in a mysterious way . . ." is from Coker, p. 11. (Coker was quoting the hymn "God Moves in a Mysterious Way," by William Cowper, which was published in 1799.)
p. 22	Coker, "Oh! my soul . . ." is from Coker, p. 14.
pp. 22–23	Coker, "I stood on deck . . ." and "The sight of them . . ." are from Coker, p. 21.
p. 23	Coker, "[N]one but those who have seen . . ." is from Coker, p. 25.
p. 24	Coker, "Had we about ten thousand . . ." is from Coker, p. 40.
pp. 25–26	Lucas, "I. may state to you. . . ." is quoted in Tyler-McGraw, p. 368.
p. 26	Johnson, "Two years long have I sought . . ." is quoted in West, p. 116.
p. 27	Ashmun, "pressed shoulder to shoulder . . ." is from Ashmun, pp. 28–29.
p. 27	Ashmun, "the destructive power . . ." is from Ashmun, p. 28.
p. 28	Ashmun, "state of utter abandonment . . ." is from Ashmun, p. 31.
p. 31	Williams, "Liberia, like all other countries . . ." is from Williams, p. 144.
p. 34	Richardson, "We have been married five years . . ." is quoted in Shick, p. 14.

CHAPTER FOUR

AMERICANS

p. 35	"The neatly painted white cottages . . ." is from Charles W. Thomas, p. 122.
p. 38	James Skipwith, "the walls of Jerusalem" and "is the Best Country . . ." are quoted in Shick, p. 53.
p. 39	Minor, "pork, beef, . . . mackerel . . ." is quoted in Wiley, p. 30.
pp. 39–40	James Skipwith, "God intended Africa . . ." is quoted in Shick, p. 53.
p. 40	Hawkins, "Our house scarcely shelters us . . ." is from a letter written by Hawkins to the American Colonization Society, July 26, 1836, in the American Colonization Society Collection, Library of Congress.
p. 41	"Here we enjoy the same rights . . ." is quoted in Wiley, p. 9.
p. 43	Bell, "call themselves *Americans*," and "all take great pride . . ." are from Bell, p. 291.
p. 45	"the best way to civilize these Natives . . ." and "I wonder to think . . ." are quoted in McCall, pp. 167–68.
p. 46	Peyton Skipwith, "It is something strange . . ." is quoted in Wiley, p. 4.

CHAPTER FIVE
LIFE UPRIVER

p. 48	Ashmun, "The cultivation of your rich lands . . ." is quoted in Gurley, p. 63.
pp. 50–51	Burke, "For four or five months . . ." is quoted in Wiley, p. 190.
p. 51	"is a coarse, tough, clammy, tasteless root . . ." is from Nesbit, p. 25.
p. 51	"Millions of coffee trees . . ." is quoted in Kimber, p. 279.
pp. 52–53	Bell, "Here are a number of farms . . ." and "The ground is undulating . . ." are from Bell, pp. 290–91.
p. 54	Dongey, "contains more than 1000 houses . . ." is quoted in Shick, p. 92.
p. 54	"War! war's come" is from a letter written by Leon Harris to the American Colonization Society, April 16, 1840, in the American Colonization Society Collection, Library of Congress.
p. 58	"the language, the manners, the habits . . ." is quoted in McCall, p. 170.

CHAPTER SIX
PROGRESS

p. 60	Blake, "by criminal conversation . . ." is from a letter written by Blake to the American Colonization Society, May 13, 1835, in the American Colonization Society Collection, Library of Congress.
p. 61	"an offensive attempt . . ." is quoted in Kennedy, p. 120.
p. 62	"grinding oppression . . ." is quoted in Starobin, p. 168.
p. 62	"In some parts of that country . . ." and "In coming to the barbarous shores . . ." are quoted in Diagram Group, p. 83.
p. 64	Matilda Skipwith, "he fell to sleep in Jesus Arms . . ." is quoted in Miller, p. 103.
p. 66	Roberts, "The time has been when men. . ." and "that all-gracious Providence . . ." are quoted in Armistead, p. 11.
p. 67	"the skill, industry and ingenuity . . ." is from *Report of the Committee*, p. 5.
p. 70	"Here food and drink we find . . ." is quoted in Shick, p. 71.

CHAPTER SEVEN
"SOME FERTILE COUNTRY"

p. 71	Wright, "It is the duty of all men . . ." is quoted in John L. Thomas, p. 11.
p. 75	Washington, "ever [to] find a home on earth . . ." is quoted in Shumard, p. 8.
p. 75	Washington, "I abhor with intense hatred . . ." is quoted in Shumard, p. 6.
p. 75	Douglass, "twin-sister of slavery . . ."; "He, if any one . . ."; and "We want colored men . . ." are quoted in "But Will They Go?" p. 292.
p. 76	Lincoln, "If all earthly power . . ." is quoted in Wesley, p. 9.
p. 76	Lincoln, "If slavery is not wrong . . ." is quoted in Steers, p. 4.
p. 78	"thousands of people dying . . ." is quoted in Marten, p. 130.
p. 78	Lincoln, "I think your race suffer . . ." is from Lincoln, p. 371.
p. 78	Chase, "How much better . . ." is quoted in Shick, p. 129.
p. 81	Lincoln, "thenceforward, and forever free," is from the Emancipation Proclamation, reprinted in Sandburg, p. 345.
p. 82	Hays, "I am glad the President . . ." and "a hideous & barbarous humbug . . ." are quoted in Scheips, p. 439.
pp. 82–84	Lincoln, "I can hardly believe . . ." is quoted in Wesley, p. 20.

CHAPTER EIGHT
"THE BECLOUDED SUN"

pp. 85–86   Roberts, "Liberia, in her progress . . ." is quoted in Blyden, pp. 8–9.

p. 86   Benson, "a glorious future for Liberia . . ." is quoted in "Forty-Fourth Annual Report," p. 84.

p. 87   Headen, "I could hardly believe my eyes . . ." is quoted in Sterling, p. 15.

pp. 87–88   "This is not the condition of really free men" is quoted in Foner, p. 62.

p. 90   Humphreys, "Ours is, and it ever shall be . . ." is quoted in Golay, p. 63.

p. 92   "a carnival of murders . . ." is quoted in Franklin, p. 163.

p. 93   Turner, "I would make Africa a place of refuge . . ." is quoted in Redkey, p. 33.

p. 93   Turner, "There is no more doubt . . ." is quoted in Redkey, p. 29.

pp. 93–94   Turner, "was not only to bear a load . . ." is quoted in Tindall, p. 160.

p. 96   Blyden, "We are keeping these lands . . ." is quoted in Shick, p. 122.

pp. 96–97   Brawley, "come to America to be educated . . ."; "The comparative isolation . . ."; and "[F]or them especially . . ." are from Brawley, pp. 208–209.

EPILOGUE
LIBERIA, TROUBLED LAND

p. 102   Tubman, "strive with all my might . . ." is quoted in Shick, p. 142.

p. 105   Doe, "The unemployment situation . . ." is quoted in Umoden, p. 13.

p. 106   "steal, kill, and destroy" is quoted in a profile of Liberian journalist Kenneth Best on the Web site of the International Press Institute: http://freemedia.at/IPIReport2.00/04Best.htm.

pp. 108-109   "We are afraid and suffering . . ." is quoted in Farah, p. A9.

p. 111   "There are still Liberians . . ." is from Dolo, p. 175.

SELECTED BIBLIOGRAPHY

Alexander, Archibald. *A History of Colonization on the Western Coast of Africa*. New York: Negro Universities Press, 1969.

Armistead, Wilson. *Calumny Refuted, by Facts from Liberia*. London: Charles Gilpin, 1848.

Ashmun, Jehudi. *History of the American Colony in Liberia: From December 1821 to 1823*. Washington, D.C.: Way & Gideon, 1826.

Bell, Charles H. "Letter from Captain Bell." *African Repository, and Colonial Journal*, October 1, 1840, pp. 289–296.

Blyden, Edward W., ed. *A Brief Account of Proceedings on the Occasion of the Retirement of President J. J. Roberts, and the Inauguration of Hon: S. A. Benson, January 7, 1856*. Liberia: G. Killian, 1856.

Boley, G. E. Saigbe. *Liberia: The Rise and Fall of the First Republic*. New York: St. Martin's Press, 1984.

Brawley, Benjamin. *A Social History of the American Negro*. London: Collier Books, 1921.

Brodie, Fawn M. *Thomas Jefferson: An Intimate History*. New York: W. W. Norton and Company, 1974.

"But will they go?" *African Repository*, October 1850, pp. 289–94.

Coker, Daniel. *Journal of Daniel Coker, a Descendent of Africa*. . . . Baltimore: E. J. Coale, 1820.

d'Azevedo, Warren L. "A Tribal Reaction to Nationalism (Part 1)." *Liberian Studies Journal*, Spring 1969, pp. 1–21.

Diagram Group. *Peoples of West Africa*. New York: Facts On File, 1997.

Dolo, Emmanuel. *Democracy Versus Dictatorship: The Quest for Freedom and Justice in Africa's Oldest Republic—Liberia*. Lanham, Md.: University Press of America, 1996.

Ellis, George W. *Negro Culture in West Africa: A Social Study of the Negro Group of Vai-Speaking People*. . . . New York: Neale Publishing Co., 1914.

Farah, Douglas. "Fighting Flares in Liberia and Threatens Ivory Coast." *Washington Post*, August 6, 2001, pp. A9, A11.

Foner, Eric, and Olivia Mahoney. *America's Reconstruction: People and Politics After the Civil War*. New York: HarperPerennial, 1995.

"Forty-Fourth Annual Report of the American Colonization Society." *African Repository*, March 1861, pp. 65–84.

Franklin, John Hope. *Reconstruction After the Civil War*. Second edition. Chicago: University of Chicago Press, 1994.

—— and Alfred A. Moss, Jr. *From Slavery to Freedom: A History of Negro Americans*. 6th edition. New York: McGraw-Hill, 1988.

Freehling, William W. "The Founding Fathers and Slavery." *American Historical Review*, February 1972, pp. 81–93.

Golay, Michael. *Reconstruction and Reaction: The Emancipation of Slaves, 1861–1913*. New York: Facts On File, 1996.

Gurley, Ralph Randolph. *Life of Jehudi Ashmun, Late Colonial Agent in Liberia*. New York: Robinson & Franklin, 1839.

Harris, Sheldon H. *Paul Cuffe: Black America and the African Return*. New York: Simon and Schuster, 1972.

Huberich, Charles Henry. *The Political and Legislative History of Liberia*. Vol. 1. New York: Central Book Company, 1947.

Jefferson, Thomas. *Notes on the State of Virginia*. New York: Harper & Row, 1964.

Johnson, Denis. "The Civil War in Hell." *Esquire*, December 1990, pp. 43–46, 219–21.

Jones, Thomas H. *The Experience and Personal Narrative of Uncle Tom Jones, Who Was for Forty Years a Slave*. Boston: Farwell & Co., 1858.

Kennedy, John P. *African Colonization—Slave Trade—Commerce*. Washington, D.C.: Gales and Seaton, 1843.

Kimber, Thomas. "Present State of Liberia." *The Friend*, June 3, 1837, pp. 278–279.

Liberian Writing: Liberia as Seen by Her Own Writers as Well as by German Authors. Tübingen, Federal Republic of Germany: Horst Erdmann Verlag, 1970.

Lincoln, Abraham. "Address on Colonization to a Deputation of Negroes," in *The Collected Works of Abraham Lincoln*, Vol. 5, *1861–1862*, edited by Roy P. Basler. New Brunswick, N.J.: Rutgers University Press, 1953.

Marten, James. *The Children's Civil War*. Chapel Hill, N.C.: University of North Carolina Press, 1998.

McCall, Daniel F., Norman R. Bennett, and Jeffrey Butler, eds. *Western African History*. New York: Frederick A. Praeger, 1969.

Miller, Randall M., ed. *"Dear Master": Letters of a Slave Family*. Ithaca, N.Y.: Cornell University Press, 1978.

Nesbit, William. *Four Months in Liberia; or, African Colonization Exposed*. Pittsburgh: J. T. Shyrock, 1855 (reprinted in *Two Black Views of Liberia*. New York: Arno Press, 1969).

Quarles, Benjamin. *Lincoln and the Negro*. New York: Oxford University Press, 1962.

Redkey, Edwin S. *Black Exodus: Black Nationalist and Back-to-Africa Movements, 1890–1910*. New Haven: Yale University Press, 1969.

The Report of the Committee of Adjudication, of the National Fair, of the Republic of Liberia. Monrovia: G. Killian, 1858.

Sandburg, Carl. *Abraham Lincoln: The Prairie Years and the War Years*. New York: Harcourt, Brace and Co., 1954.

Scheips, Paul J. "Lincoln and the Chiriqui Colonization Project." *The Journal of Negro History*, October 1952, pp. 418–453.

Sherwood, Henry Noble. "The Formation of the American Colonization Society." *The Journal of Negro History*, July 1917, pp. 209–28.

—— ."Paul Cuffe and His Contribution to the American Colonization Society," in *Proceedings of the Mississippi Valley Historical Association, 1912–1913*, edited by Benjamin F. Shambaugh. Cedar Rapids, Ia.: The Torch Press, 1913.

Shick, Tom W. *Behold the Promised Land: A History of Afro-American Settler Society in Nineteenth-Century Liberia*. Baltimore: The Johns Hopkins University Press, 1980.

Shumard, Ann M. *A Durable Memento: Portraits by Augustus Washington, African American Daguerreotypist*. Washington, D.C.: Smithsonian Institution, 1999.

Smith, James Wesley. *Sojourners in Search of Freedom: The Settlement of Liberia by Black Americans*. Lanham, Md.: University Press of America, 1987.

Starobin, Robert S., ed. *Blacks in Bondage: Letters of American Slaves*. New York: Markus Wiener Publishing, 1988.

Steers, Edward, Jr. "Great Emancipator or Grand Wizard?" Review of *Forced into Glory: Abraham Lincoln's White Dream*, by Lerone Bennett, Jr. (Chicago: Johnson Publishing Co., 2000). First published in the Springfield, Ill., *State-Journal Register*, June 25, 2000. *Abraham Lincoln Online*, http://showcase.netins.net/web/creative/lincoln/books/steers.htm, June 21, 2001.

Sterling, Dorothy, ed. *The Trouble They Seen: The Story of Reconstruction in the Words of African Americans*. New York: Da Capo Press, 1994.

Thomas, Charles W. *Adventures and Observations on the West Coast of Africa, and Its Islands.* New York: Derby & Jackson, 1860.

Thomas, John L. *Slavery Attacked: The Abolitionist Crusade.* Englewood Cliffs, N.J.: Spectrum Books, 1965.

Tindall, George Brown. *South Carolina Negroes.* Columbia, S.C.: University of South Carolina Press, 1952.

Tyler-McGraw, Marie, ed. "'The Prize I Mean Is the Prize of Liberty': A Loudoun County Family in Liberia." *Virginia Magazine of History and Biography,* July 1989, pp. 355–74.

Umoden, Gabriel E. *The Liberian Crisis: A Photographic Expedition.* Lagos, Nigeria: Gabumo Publishing Co., 1992.

Walker, David. *Walker's Appeal, in Four Articles, Together with a Preamble.* 2nd ed. Boston: D. Walker, 1830.

Wesley, Charles H. "Lincoln's Plan for Colonizing the Emancipated Negroes." *The Journal of Negro History,* January 1919, pp. 7–20.

West, Richard. *Back to Africa: A History of Sierra Leone and Liberia.* London: Jonathan Cape, 1970.

Wiley, Bell I., ed. *Slaves No More: Letters from Liberia, 1833–1869.* Lexington, Ky.: University of Kentucky Press, 1980.

Williams, Samuel. *Four Years in Liberia,* in *Liberian Dreams: Back-to-Africa Narratives from the 1850s,* edited by Wilson Jeremiah Moses. University Park, Pa.: The Pennsylvania State University Press, 1998.

Note: Page numbers in *italic* type refer to illustrations.